Internal Marketing

Your Company's Next Stage of Growth

HAWORTH Marketing Resources
Innovations in Practice & Professional Services
William J. Winston, Senior Editor

New, Recent, and Forthcoming Titles:

Marketing for Churches and Ministries by Robert E. Stevens and David L. Loudon

The Clinician's Guide to Managed Mental Health Care by Norman Winegar

Framework for Market-Based Hospital Pricing Decisions by Shahram Heshmat

Professional Services Marketing: Strategy and Tactics by F. G. Crane

A Guide to Preparing Cost-Effective Press Releases by Robert H. Loeffler

How to Create Interest-Evoking, Sales-Inducing, Non-Irritating Advertising by Walter Weir

Market Analysis: Assessing Your Business Opportunities by Robert E. Stevens, Philip K. Sherwood, and J. Paul Dunn

Selling Without Confrontation by Jack Greening

Persuasive Advertising for Entrepreneurs and Small Business Owners: How to Create More Effective Sales Messages by Jay P. Granat

Marketing Mental Health Services to Managed Care by Norman Winegar and John L. Bistline

New Product Screening: A Step-Wise Approach by William C. Lesch and David Rupert

Church and Ministry Strategic Planning: From Concept to Success by R. Henry Migliore, Robert E. Stevens, and David L. Loudon

Business in Mexico: Managerial Behavior, Protocol, and Etiquette by Candace Bancroft McKinniss and Arthur A. Natella

Managed Service Restructuring–A Strategic Approach in a Competitive Environment by Robert L. Goldman and Sanjib K. Mukherjee

A Marketing Approach to Physician Recruitment by James Hacker, Don C. Dodson, and M. Thane Forthman

Marketing for CPAs, Accountants, and Tax Professionals edited by William J. Winston

Strategic Planning for Not-for-Profit Organizations by R. Henry Migliore, Robert E. Stevens, and David L. Loudon

Marketing Planning in a Total Quality Environment by Robert E. Linneman and John L. Stanton, Jr.

Managing Sales Professionals: The Reality of Profitability by Joseph P. Vaccaro

Publicity for Mental Health Clinicians: Using TV, Radio, and Print Media to Enhance Your Public Image by Douglas H. Ruben

Squeezing a New Service into a Crowded Market by Dennis J. Cahill

Managing a Public Relations Firm for Growth and Profit by A. C. Croft

Internal Marketing: Your Company's Next Stage of Growth by Dennis J. Cahill

Internal Marketing

Your Company's Next Stage of Growth

Dennis J. Cahill

Routledge
Taylor & Francis Group
NEW YORK AND LONDON

First Published by 1996 The Haworth Press, Inc.,
10 Alice Street, Binghamton, NY 13904-1580

This edition published 2010 by Routledge
711 Third Avenue, New York, NY 10017
2 Park Square, Milton Park, Abingdon, Oxfordshire OX14 4RN

First issued in paperback 2016

Routledge is an imprint of the Taylor and Francis Group, an informa business

Library of Congress Cataloging-in-Publication Data

Cahill, Dennis J.
Internal marketing : your company's next stage of growth / Dennis J. Cahill.
p. cm.
Includes bibliographical references and index.
ISBN 0-7890-6005-1 (alk. paper)
1. Marketing—Management. 2. Marketing channels. 3. Market segmentation. I. Title.
HF5415.13.C25 1996
658.8—dc20 95-35020
CIP

Publisher's Note
The publisher has gone to great lengths to ensure the quality of this reprint but points out that some imperfections in the original may be apparent.

ISBN 13: 978-1-138-97298-8 (pbk)
ISBN 13: 978-0-7890-6005-1 (hbk)

To the memory of my sister
Laurie Patricia Cahill
1944-1995

ABOUT THE AUTHOR

Dennis J. Cahill, MBA, MA, has headed North Union Associates, Inc., a finance, investment, and marketing consulting firm in Cleveland, Ohio, since 1983. He founded the firm after almost a decade of increasingly responsible financial positions held in the cement and banking industries. Mr. Cahill has also taught undergraduate and graduate marketing and finance courses at three Cleveland area colleges. He has published numerous articles in scholarly and professional publications and has spoken at national professional conferences and local meetings. In October, 1992, he was appointed editor of the *Journal of Product and Brand Management.* While heading North Union Associates, Mr. Cahill has been active in many aspects of new product and new service development, from initial concept through delivery of completed product to end user. He is a member of the American Marketing Association, the Academy of Management, the Association of Psychological Type, the Association for Consumer Research, the Cleveland Business Economists Club, and The Barnard Society, USA.

CONTENTS

Preface

This is no longer the book that I set out to write. Although I am sure that this is not an unusual experience for authors, it was not my experience when I wrote *Squeezing a New Service into a Crowded Market.* This book started out as a rather straight-forward book on internal marketing–at least as I viewed the subject–but has veered toward being an unorthodox book on the subject. I grew increasingly concerned as I did the research on the topic that marketers have focused too narrowly on the subject, closing off substantial areas in which an application of a more general conception would be of great benefit. *That* is the book which I hopc I havc written.

This is a work that is intended both for practitioners of the art of services marketing as well as for advanced marketing students interested in the "real-world" application of some of the marketing theory they have been exposed to. As such, it sits at the intersection of two normally separate disciplines: marketing–especially services marketing, and organizational sciences–especially organizational behavior. The practitioners and academics from these two disciplines normally do not interact with each other very much, if at all; normally marketers do not read the organizational literature, nor do "organizational scientists" read the marketing material. However, because of how my consulting practice has developed over the past decade I have had to read voluminously in many byways in both areas and have made the connections that appear in this book. They are here so that you, the reader, do not have to dig through the arcane, academic language in which much of the material has been written in order to make your own connections.

A roadmap of the direction of the book should prove helpful. Chapter 1 discusses all the definitions of internal marketing as well as why internal marketing is necessary, even in smaller firms. Chapter 2 discusses what the internal marketing program should actually market. Chapter 3 enlarges on the theme of to whom to market through a discussion of segmentation strategies and schemes. Chapter 4 examines the "how"–communication strategies and methods as well as various models that have been used by service firms in the past to achieve a level of internal marketing; the chapter continues with a discussion of "Learning Organizations" and how this relatively new concept needs to relate to internal marketing. Next, Chapter 4 develops a new model that better describes the relationships and activities necessary to achieve the necessary new level of internal marketing for the twenty-first century. Chapter 5 looks at the specific application of an internal marketing program to the question of innovation and how to manage innovation successfully. Chapter 6 delves into what will be gained by a firm in implementing an internal marketing program. There are two appendixes at the end: the first has the addresses and phone numbers of the organizations mentioned in the text, for easy reference; the second is a fairly technical discussion of marketing typologies, their uses and applications.

All authors have too many debts to acknowledge. Often we stand on the shoulders of giants, which makes seeing farther easy. In my case there are few giants. Ordinary people have helped my intellectual development through the years, from my early days as a history graduate student, through my MBA days and including several people for whom I worked, who would never claim to have fostered anything remotely intellectual. Several individuals must be mentioned by name, however, for specific help with the present work. Dr. Leonard Berry generously provided encouragement at the book's inception. Dr. Sharon Thach, Dr. Robert Hisrich, Steven Verba, and Robert M. Warshawsky read early drafts of some of the material; Harold Douthit contributed material and consulting jobs from time to time which have made working on this book easier.

Editors, book-review editors, and anonymous reviewers of several journals need to be thanked for their comments on papers and articles which presented earlier forms of some of the material presented herein. Some of these were published, some were not, but all the comments were valuable and were considered, whether changed or not: *Journal of Consumer Marketing, International Journal of Research in Marketing, Journal of Consumer Research, Pricing: Strategy and Practice, Academy of Management Executive, Academy of Management Journal, Academy of Management Review, Marketing News, Services Marketing Today, Journal of Marketing, Environment and Behavior, Journal of Business-to-Business Marketing, Journal of Professional Services Marketing, Journal of Customer Service in Marketing and Management, Journal of Business and Industrial Marketing, Journal of Services Marketing, The Journal of Product Innovation Marketing, European Journal of Marketing,* and *Family Business Review.* Reviewers of the late Services Marketing Conference of the American Marketing Association, the High-Technology Management Conference of the University of Colorado, the Association of Private Enterprise Education Conference, and the Small-Business Institute Directors Association Conference also offered comments upon several papers.

And, of course, thanks to my wife Jeanine and children Abigail and Teddy for understanding when I was abstracted or missing.

Dennis J. Cahill

Chapter 1

Definitions and Necessities

What is "Internal Marketing?" Why is it important? Is it a concept that is unique, or of unique importance, only to services-marketing firms, the context in which it is usually cited? And how does internal marketing differ from simply an internal application of the venerable Marketing Concept of the Introduction to Marketing textbooks?

MARKETING CONCEPT

The Marketing Concept is not new. It is now almost 40 years since John McKitterick (1957) put forth the idea that the Marketing Concept is a customer-oriented, integrated, profit-oriented philosophy of business. In the ensuing years, while there has been profound debate on the idea (e.g., Hirschman, 1983), the *concept* has survived. An undergraduate marketing text taken at random from my bookshelves devotes two pages of explanation and a chart to the Marketing Concept explaining–with little change from McKitterick–that it is a "customer-oriented, integrated, goal-oriented philosophy for a firm, institution, or person" (Evans and Berman, 1987:12-14).

One would expect that any concept so basic as to appear in an introductory textbook would be wholeheartedly subscribed to by practitioners and academics alike. In the case of the Marketing Concept, however, nothing could be further from the truth. Again, to sample my files at random, Hirschman (1983:45) proposes that the concept is not applicable to artists and ideologists because of "the personal values and social norms that characterize the production process" of these persons' output. Berry (1988:28), in an article aimed at practitioners, states that the Marketing Concept "will continue to gain in importance and application." Hampton and Lane (1982) state that the Marketing Concept is anathema to at least a large portion of the employees in the newspaper industry. John C. Crawford (1983:450) states that the Marketing Concept "appears to be an impossible philosophy to put into effect. . . . [It] is still loudly proclaimed but seldom seen. It represents the unattainable–the marketing utopia."

I have written often before to defend the Marketing Concept. Cahill (1992b and 1992c) takes a relatively lighthearted and untraditional look at ways to organize successful marketing efforts around the concept; Cahill (1992a); Cahill, Thach and Warshawsky (1994) look at the Marketing Concept as a way to prevent over-innovativeness to the detriment of client needs in professional service firms. Cahill and Warshawsky (1993) reiterate the importance of the concept even in high technology products, stating that these types of products are not exempt from the workings of consumer behavior which drives the Marketing Concept, despite the feelings of all too many people that high tech is immune from these considerations. Cahill, Warshawsky, and Thach (1994) similarly reiterate this fact, using the fate of two computer software programs as case studies. Thus, with this background of thought and writing on the subject of the Marketing Concept (rather extensive on a somewhat philosophical topic for a nonacademic), I am hardly "objective" on the subject, much less dispassionate. I strongly believe that the Marketing Concept, properly understood and correctly implemented, is one of the basic tools in the marketer's tool kit. Without the Marketing Concept, good marketing–internal or external–is difficult, if not impossible.

INTERNAL MARKETING

Although there are earlier definitions of internal marketing–which will be detailed and discussed later in this chapter–what I consider to be the basic definition is enunciated by Leonard L. Berry and A. Parasuraman in their book *Marketing Services: Competing Through Quality* (1991:151):

> Internal marketing is attracting, developing, motivating, and retaining qualified employees through job-products that satisfy their needs. Internal marketing is the *philosophy* of treating employees as customers–indeed, "wooing" employees . . .–and is the *strategy* of shaping job-products to fit human needs.

Although this definition is compact, it says quite a lot, and says it in unmistakable terms of focusing on employees and their needs. But it sounds less like marketing and more like something out of a text on human resources management. Indeed, in a critique of internal marketing as a concept–not aimed specifically at Berry and Parasuraman's definition–Rafiq and Ahmed (1993) attempt to draw a boundary around human resources management and tell the marketing profession to butt out. The reason for Rafiq and Ahmed's concern is reflected in articles such as Bak et al. (1994:38) which specifically define internal marketing as using "a marketing perspective for managing an organization's human resources." Bak et al. then retreat somewhat from this imperialistic statement by rather lamely stating that the premise of internal marketing is that "internal exchanges between the organization and its employee groups must be operating effectively before the organization can be successful in achieving its goals regarding external markets"–a statement with which few modern managers would quarrel, but one which has little empirical support. Further, an anonymous reviewer of an early draft of one of the papers upon which some of this book is based defined internal marketing as "good human resource management with a view to satisfying external customers"–exactly the sort of expansive definition that worries Rafiq and Ahmed. In short, although Rafiq and Ahmed would probably approve of a market-driven organization, they are very concerned that such not turn into a marketing-driven organization.

Potential definitions of internal marketing are practically endless; I will provide only a very small sample of the definitions that have sprung up in the academic literature in the past decade. Johnson and Seymour (1985:226) state that internal marketing should "create an internal environment which supports customer-consciousness and sales-mindedness" among the personnel. Johnson, Scheuing, and Gaida (1986:140) define it as a "service firm's efforts to provide all members of the organization with a clear understanding of the corporate mission and objectives and with the training, motivation, and evaluation to achieve the desired objectives." George (1990), echoing Berry and Parasuraman above, describes internal marketing as a philosophy for managing the organization's human resources based on a marketing perspective.

But the grandfather of all definitions is probably Gronroos (1981a, 1981b): "Selling the firm to the employees" who are treated as "internal customers." The thought here is that the higher employee satisfaction that will result will make it possible to develop a more customer-focused and market-oriented firm. Gronroos then deals with strategic levels (1981a) and tactical levels (1981b) of internal marketing. In a more recent article on the subject, Gronroos (1994:13) states that the "internal marketing *concept*" asserts that

> the internal market of employees is best motivated for service mindedness and customer-oriented performance by an active, marketing-like approach, where a variety of activities are used internally in an active, marketinglike and coordinated way.

In short, internal marketing in its currently accepted guise is a philosophy of managing a relatively large service firm so that the employees are treated as customers by each other, since so often service encounters are dealt with by a succession of employees. This definition is all well and good, but too exclusive; and by its exclusiveness misses several opportunities to present itself as a central aspect of all firms.

First, the current definitions more or less miss the fact that organizations in our economic system exist to meet customer needs by selling goods and/or services to those customers. (I almost said "providing"–following the tenor of the current literature–but none of the approximately 60 definitions in my on-line thesaurus nor the dozens in my hard-copy Roget's uses "sell" as a synonym for "provide" and I wish to focus on the exchange of services for money later on.)

Second, the definitions miss the fact that the organization must focus outward to the market, not inward to the employees. No matter how internal to an organization a service seems to be–providing computer support to the firm's employees, for example–focusing on those "customers" and forgetting that there are customers beyond them outside, may lead to disaster.

Third, the definitions focus too exclusively on service firms. Although there has been a continued blurring of lines between service and manufacturing firms in recent years, with more manufacturing firms talking about how good their "service" has become, there are differences between service firms and others. Nevertheless, an expanded definition of internal marketing will encompass the same tasks at both types of firms; many of these tasks are as necessary in service firms as they are in manufacturing firms.

Fourth, these definitions miss what is probably the most important aspect of internal marketing–the fact that it is a practice of communication with employees. It is essential to let them know what is going on so they can do their jobs effectively and efficiently so the external customers and the internal customers are well served by the organization. They must also know which activities are acceptable and which are not. In short, the employees must be treated as *partners*–not customers–in the firm's effort to provide goods and services to the buying public.

Fifth, as Randall and McCullough (1991) so bluntly point out, there is a difference between the internal marketing *concept* and internal marketing *programs*. Many firms may pay lip service to the internal marketing concept, as they do to so many other concepts and hot management ideas that are reported in the business press, but few firms become truly dedicated to putting programs into place because of the expense of time, energy, and money. When the crunch comes between "moving iron out the door" and doing what needs to be done to improve the work force so customer needs can be taken care of, all too often iron moves out the door. Period.

WHY INTERNAL MARKETING?

This is, after all, why firms practice internal marketing–to make our external customers happy with us so they will continue to buy our goods and services. In fact, Compton et al. (1987:10) bluntly state that an "internal action program is a prerequisite for successful external marketing." If the outside customer can get better service because of your internal marketing efforts, they will come back for more of what you are selling. This is true whether we are talking about a professional service firm, such as a law firm or an accounting firm; a service firm, such as a bank or a fast-food chain; a manufacturer, such as Chrysler or Apple Computer; a nonprofit entity such as a hospital or the Girl Scouts; or a governmental agency, such as the Postal Service or the municipal recreation department. If your internal marketing efforts do not deliver better services to your external customers, then every dollar spent on internal marketing, every minute of management time spent, will have been wasted. And, as Davidow (1986:53-70) reminds us, serviceability must be incorporated into the design from the beginning; good service is a strategic problem and starts at the top; bad service costs the firm money but good service earns it; and it is possible to segment customers on the basis of the service that they wish to receive. And as Rathnam, Mahahan, and Whinston (1994) report, it is now possible, with help from currently available technology, to design customer support teams and processes to produce effective coordination and customer satisfaction.

Grove and Fisk (1989, 1992) have opened a new metaphorical door by using drama to describe the service encounter. I want to open the door wider by expanding this metaphor to include its use in internal marketing situations. I will do so in some detail in Chapter 4; however, I would like to use this metaphor here to explain why we do internal marketing. Since a part of the firm's "back office" provides services (either to the firm's front region or to another portion of the back region) the back office also has a metaphorical front and a back region, overlapping in nature and potentially quite damaging. If the back office does not practice marketing internally, then the areas of the firm to which they provide services will resist–to the extent possible–"purchasing" services from them, no matter the corporate rationale for so doing. And the corporate rationale may be compelling. Nevertheless, if the back office does not follow the dictates of the Marketing Concept and does not expand upon that dictum by practicing internal marketing, all of the corporate compulsion will produce only sullen compliance at best.

I worked in the Trust Administration Department of a large bank for a number of years before moving to a smaller bank. As part of the recruitment effort, it had been made clear that I would be in charge of bringing the record-keeping function of the smaller bank's savings plan in-house and dealing with the bank's personnel department about the transition. I set up an introductory meeting among the current record-keeping firm, the trust department, and personnel. A very senior vice-president of personnel attended–without coat, feet upon the conference room table while waiting for the record-keeping firm's people to arrive (quite in keeping with his normal behavior). This individual's work contacts were almost totally "back office" in nature and he was used to being backstage but never onstage before an audience. Internal marketing as a concept, however, states that *everyone* is always onstage, even if it is only before an audience of fellow employees and not before a "real" customer. (In fact, this contrast of "fellow employees" with "real customers"–so frequent in actual firms–is fraught with danger; our fellow employees *are* our real customers, if we are support personnel.) In contrast, I was used to being "front office" a major portion of the time, meeting with customers and other outside service providers, and only went "backstage" for support services. This meeting turned out to be a disaster–primarily, it seems to me, because of this staging problem.

It is this point of internal *versus* external customers that seems to me to be both a strength of the internal marketing concept and one of its causes of confusion: few employees serve both external and internal customers. If we are support personnel, we rarely see an outside customer; if we deal with outside customers, we rarely deal with other employees as a *provider*–we are *users* of support services. Therefore, internal marketing may seem, to those who face outward, like a cheerleading session for support personnel and thus beneath their notice. "Customer-contact personnel" tend to have higher status in service firms, senior management tends to come from the contact area, not support; thus the customer-contact mentality tends to dominate such firms.

Internal marketing programs need, of course, to tie the two areas together with very strong bonds; it is this part of the "good human resource management with a view to satisfying external customers" statement denigrated above that makes sense. But whose vision of the firm is correct? Which vision is to govern? I would like to suggest a novel approach, one which (in different circumstances and to a different end) I suggested in *Squeezing a New Service into a Crowded Marketplace* (Cahill, 1995): Do some perceptual mapping analyses of your market. Internal marketing is not an end in itself; we practice internal marketing only so that we can do a better job of marketing externally. Find out what your external customers want; find out what your employees want; see where these wants, needs, and possibilities overlap. Management's vision of the firm may not be what the customers of the firm want; management's vision would need to change. The section in Chapter 6 on learning organizations offers reasons that seem to be imperative about how to develop a vision shared by the entire organization.

HOW DO WE PRACTICE INTERNAL MARKETING?

And how do we practice internal marketing? Before exploring full-blown, modern internal marketing programs, I would like to discuss two tried-and-true methods that are often overlooked in the rush to be stylish. Cross selling programs and gainsharing programs have been around for decades, both in service firms and manufacturing firms, and have proved their worth time and time again. It does not pay to overlook their applicability simply because they seem to be outmoded. They are not.

Cross Selling

Cross selling is a term from the financial services industry, one that I have not seen used elsewhere. Simply put, it is the selling by a representative of one department–such as the retail banking department of services available from another department–such as the trust department. This is a concept much honored in the financial services industry, and for three very good reasons. First, it is unlikely that a customer knows all of the services offered by a bank; he or she may need a trust account or commercial loan, but not know how to go about obtaining the service. Second, the services provided by banks tend to be fairly uniform: a safe-deposit box is a safe-deposit box, a commercial loan is a commercial loan. Therefore, a typical bank customer may have relationships with several different institutions around town; capturing more services per customer increases the bank's profitability with very little sales effort on the bank's part. Third, the more relationships a customer has with a bank, the less likely that customer is to leave the bank (unless the provocation is intense) thus increasing the length of profitability per customer. It seems to me that looking at the operation of a cross selling program would be advantageous for all service providers. Balombin (1987) reports upon such an advantageous instance, claiming that an integrated marketing plan was largely responsible for its success.

Banks devote a lot of time and attention to cross selling programs, as successful cross selling efforts are immensely profitable. Cash and noncash incentives to employees for landing new accounts from existing customers are frequently large. I left Central National Bank's trust department in November, 1982 for Society National Bank, which had a departmental incentive fund for new trust accounts. Although I was in the department for less than two months, my incentive check was enough for me to buy a new suit. While I was at Central, around 1980, I participated in a bank-wide program to increase core deposits and won a slide-projector and other awards worth over $400. Nevertheless, there are problems inherent in these efforts that affect both employee morale and the profitability of the new accounts and changed relationships.

First is the fact that not every employee has equal professional contact with outside customers and prospects. This leads to potentially great possibilities of unfairness in incentive awards. The method Society used to lessen the problem was that half of the cash-incentive pot was divided based upon the percentage of an individual's salary to the departmental total; the other half was divided based upon how much business an individual brought in. The only drawback in this method was that most of the lower-salaried individuals in the department also had little outside contact, so they had little chance for much money—but at least everyone got a couple hundred dollars or so. A potential morale problem—one that plagues many services firms and not just banks—is low pay. Although low pay can be an ongoing source of irritation to employees, what can happen during an incentive program can be devastating. One of the trust department clerks applied for a MasterCard during the above-mentioned program because we earned points for each card issued that we had solicited. But Fred was turned down for the card *because he did not earn enough to qualify*. The irony of the disqualification was not lost on anyone in the trust department.

Second is the fact that bankers and other professionals frequently resent having to sell and rarely know how to do it well. Over time, an individual may learn through osmosis how to sell the primary service in the department, but this does not mean that the employee either knows how nor wishes to sell anything offered by another department. Frequently cross selling programs confuse selling with closing and signing business—a potential disaster.

Third, and leading from the second point, is the fact that in a company-wide program, dividing the incentive becomes difficult. Does the program split the incentive payment for introducing a prospect to another department? In half or some other way? Does the introducer get half credit even if the supposed closer upsets the prospect and loses the account? Is the introducer expected to close a sale for a service that is unknown to him or her?

Fourth, how well trained in total offerings of the firm is the work force? Based upon my several years in the banking business, I am not sanguine on this point. A large commercial bank offered dozens of different services, even in the pre-deregulation early 1980s; how was anyone supposed to keep up with this tidal wave of offerings? In a bank of that size with its typical employee turnover, it was impossible simply to know whom to call to find out what a customer might want, much less know anything about the specific service.

Fifth, how well do the personnel understand what marketing is and how it operates? It is frequently the case that the employees do not know anything about marketing as a concept and consider selling or advertising to be all that there is to marketing. This is particularly true concerning professionals such as lawyers or accountants, very "low-level" employees such as bank tellers, or employees at nonprofit institutions or governmental agencies. Compton (1987) reports on a program at a Red Cross blood center to provide the employees with a simple orientation to marketing and its concepts as a first step to a deeper internal marketing program; this is a good idea.

And yet, the potential increase in sales and profits is simply too great to let the difficulties listed above deter an organization from attempting a well-designed cross selling program. What constitutes a well-designed cross selling program? There are three elements that are absolutely essential.

First is training: training of employees at all levels in what the organization does, who does it, and how it is done. This must not be an attempt to enlarge anyone's job. Above all, this must not be an attempt to make it possible for someone to perform all the jobs in the shop; if the organization performs a complex, technical service, such a task is impossible. The training should provide the employees an understanding of all the services provided and how they mesh with each other. Then, when employees are talking with their customers or prospects, they are armed with the information necessary to enable them to show the customer how the meshing of the organization's services will provide that customer better service than if the customer assembled the same array from several service providers. The training should be delivered, not by professional trainers, but by the people who provide the service itself. They know the service better than a professional trainer could know; further, the trainees then have a person to call to help them with customers who might need the service. This training is ongoing, not something only offered during a one-month new-employee cram course. Services change, people change, and everyone needs to be refreshed from time to time about what the organization sells.

Next is management commitment to a cross selling program. Given the relatively easy increase in sales and large potential increase in profitability that cross selling can deliver, this should go without saying. However, this commitment entails costs to the organization, costs that management must be prepared for. Obviously, given the first step above, good ongoing training must be provided at all levels of the organization; despite being offered in-house, it is not free. The "trainers" need time to develop their course materials and to handle questions which will arise from others in the organization, questions that may never lead to a consummated sale. This is part of the hidden cost of cross selling; the "trainer" in each department will need to carry a reduced case load to allow for the friction on his or her time.

The third element is a compensation/incentive system. Depending upon the employees, this could be as inexpensive as providing public acknowledgment of new business acquired by individuals. One year when I was in the corporate trust department of Central National Bank, I brought in more business (based upon a Byzantine fee-scoring system which penalized the type of business I was bringing in) as a part-time salesman whose primary job was trust administration–than six of the eight full-time business development officers. This was never publicly recognized–a fact that irritated me. We were all supposed to develop business; but I was good at it, enjoyed it, and took the time to do it. More likely, the compensation/incentive system (*not* "program") will consist of cash, and probably lots of it. Although I do not remember the percentage of fee that was used in the program at Society National Bank mentioned previously, the pool of money that was divided was in the middle five figures in 1982–for a trust department that was small in number of employees and only medium-sized in assets under management. It was not impossible for an administrative officer who tried to sell his or her accounts and develop new ones based upon contacts with lawyers and accountants to get a bonus of between one-quarter and one-third of salary. Not bad incentive for those so motivated, and the public peer recognition was not bad either.

Gainsharing

Gainsharing seeks other goals, although increased profitability of the enterprise is at the heart of the concept and the typical program. What is gainsharing? Brian Graham-Moore (1990a) has defined it as follows:

> "Gainsharing involves a measurement of productivity combined with the calculation of a bonus designed to offer employees a mutual share of any increases in total organizational productivity. Usually all those responsible for the increase receive the bonus."

Kevin Paulsen (1989) has stated that gainsharing programs are an excellent way to increase teamwork, employee output (and thus pay), and the firm's profits, "because the programs reward employees for combined work efforts." A typical program "sets a goal in a dollar amount" to improve a firm's performance. Employee efforts that "increase productivity, based on a comparison of employee costs to what employees sell or produce" are rewarded monetarily and directly. In short, a gainsharing plan is profit sharing at its best: employee contributions to increased profitability of the firm are shared with the employees.

A major percentage of the gainsharing plans put into place in the past have been established in relatively large, publicly held manufacturing firms. Much of this may be attributable to the fact that the first true gainsharing plan was the Scanlon Plan, devised by Joseph Scanlon, vice president of the United Steelworkers of America. Thus, gainsharing plans have seemed most applicable in large manufacturing firms with large union involvement. Another factor favoring the establishment of gainsharing plans in relatively large firms is a widely disbursed shareholder base, giving management a greater say in the running of the firm than they might otherwise have.

Graham-Moore (1990b) made a comprehensive review of the literature on the subject. (The literature, although extensive, is somewhat hindered because of the tendency on the part of many managements to regard gainsharing information as proprietary.) Based upon the current literature, he concluded that the keys to *all* successful gainsharing plans are:

1. The normal, average, or standard labor cost is measurable;
2. The ratio of either sales value of production or units of production value to labor cost is relatively stable;
3. The policy established for sharing true increases in labor productivity is "fair."

To the extent that service enterprises present greater difficulties in these areas (because of their frequently small size and other attributes of services having precluded the sophisticated "professionalism" needed to establish cost-accounting systems or "policies" of any sort), installation of gainsharing plans in these firms may be a problem. Further studies have indicated that communication in both directions with the employees is as crucial as any of the above attributes, as is the simplicity of the plan. Paulsen (1991) outlines several lessons he has learned over the years: commitment, simplicity, involvement, and communication. Although there is no guarantee, of course, that these factors will be easier to attain in a service firm, it is to be hoped that a firm with management and ownership often in the same hands, anxious to have the improvement in profitability that gainsharing promises, would find it possible to abide by these four lessons.

What are the optimal conditions for a gainsharing plan to succeed? The list is long, but it seems that it may be summarized as follows:

1. Each plan must be custom-designed for the firm in question.
2. Competitive wage and fringe benefit programs must already be operative prior to adoption of the gainsharing plan.
3. Gainsharing must not be used as a "salvage operation," but should be installed in successful and competently managed firms.
4. Gainsharing should not be installed along with an individual incentive system because of their competing philosophies.
5. Gainsharing should include all employees at a given facility, or at least within identifiable departments or divisions.
6. Gainsharing bonuses should not be flat amounts but should vary with wages for time worked.
7. Gainsharing plan implementation requires an education program that enlists the great majority of employees.
8. Installation of any new gainsharing plan should be subject to a significant majority affirmative vote of all covered employees. Management of publicly held firms is used to dealing with this element of democracy.
9. The first year of gainsharing should be a trial period, after which future continuation of gainsharing should be contingent on one additional favorable vote by employees.
10. Termination of gainsharing should be subject to 90-day notice by management.

11. Everyone involved *must* have an understanding of the gainsharing formula, at least in its connection to performance.
12. The gainsharing formula should be monitored regularly and carefully to ensure equitable results for both the company and the employees.
13. Initial gainsharing success depends on the dedication, enthusiasm, and competence of a "champion"–such as the highest management at a facility.
14. The role of third parties in developing, disseminating, and educating in the operating facts of gainsharing is very important in the building of trust and confidence in the plan–particularly in the early years.
15. All suggestions, as well as minutes of the involvement system, *must* be open, public, and distributed so that maximum employee recognition is achieved.
16. Quality of the product should be improved as part of a plan to achieve total organization productivity. In fact, gainsharing is an ideal entry into a total redesign of the firm's strategy–in terms of its employees, its marketing, and its overall future direction.
17. The committee is a consultative or advising body, and not a decision-making one–management manages, the committee advises.
18. Rapid follow-up on the disposition of suggestions encourages employees to make more suggestions.
19. The productivity-sharing calculation, and any changes to it, must establish the bonus at a level which does not jeopardize the firm's ability to compete.
20. Bonus earnings should be paid separately from normal paychecks.

There is also a list developed by Timothy Ross (1990), a consultant in the field, of characteristics that firms whose plans *fail* exhibit to an extensive degree. Of this list, the one variable that has a dramatic impact upon many service enterprises is a poor internal financial information system. It will be imperative that management open the books to a great extent. No matter how financially unsophisticated and trusting the employees are, it is apparent that gainsharing only works well when the employees become more financially savvy and also become quasi-partners of the owners. In order for these events to occur, the owners have to trust their employees and open the books to them.

Ross quotes the results of a study conducted a few years ago of 23 firms where gainsharing had been implemented (1990). The following findings support the list above:

1. High levels of failure are associated with low levels of employee participation.
2. Larger firm size does not seem to be a major factor for failure; interestingly, Ross does not state that smaller firm size is a plus or minus factor.
3. Low levels of managerial confidence in participative management are strongly associated with failure or marginal success.
4. The longer the plan survives, the less likely that the firm will abandon it.
5. When installing a plan, realistic favorable expectations are important.
6. If a high-level executive does not take a leading role, the probability of a plan's failure increases.
7. Technology seems to have no relation to plan failure.

The upshot of the above lists and discussion, along with articles by Beck (1992), Masternak and Ross (1992), Ost (1990), and Doherty, Nord, and McAdams (1989) is that gainsharing is doable, probably should be done at most firms, and could be done in a service enterprise.

Despite the statement made above that the first year of a gainsharing plan must be understood by all concerned to be a trial period, no firm should enter the design and implementation of such a plan without the wholehearted commitment of management to live with the results of this effort for the foreseeable future. Gainsharing plans seem to be rather delicate creatures at birth, becoming quite robust, however, as they mature. One of the criteria for future longevity of a plan is current longevity: expected plan life is positively correlated with current plan age. Although this seems to be an academic tautology–defining inertia–it is not; success breeds success and should be planned for.

Goodman and Dean (1990) have developed a list of criteria which can be utilized to help ensure that any gainsharing plan lasts:

1. *Carefully select organizations.* Some reasons *not* to select a particular organization are an unstable economic environment, instability in leadership environment, and mistrust between employees and management.
2. *Plan for institutionalization from the beginning.*
3. *There must be a good organizational fit.* There needs to be a good fit between the organization's values, philosophy, and structure and the nature of the change program.
4. *Training and education in the plan must occur continuously, not just at start-up.* Gainsharing is just like the cross selling program in this regard.
5. *Commitment at all levels of the organization is necessary, especially from the top.* Again, just like cross selling.
6. *Build an effective reward system.* Include both intrinsic and extrinsic rewards linked to desired behaviors and with a mechanism for revising the system as needed over time.

A firm with a good cross selling system in place, one with gainsharing in place (with or without a formal cross selling program) should be a firm with higher than average profitability, higher return to capital, with more-satisfied customers and employees who will be less likely to depart for greener pastures. In service businesses, where often the firm's only real assets are the employees and the customer list, keeping customers and employees long-term is the only true route to long-term profitability. Any extra effort needed to retain customers and employees will probably pay large dividends, since it is notoriously more expensive to acquire new customers or employees than to keep the existing ones.

In the end, however, a firm can only be as good as its people. As Berry and Parasuraman (1991:171) state, the firms that practice internal marketing effectively will:

1. Compete aggressively for talent;
2. Offer a vision that brings purpose and meaning to the workplace;
3. Equip people with the skills and knowledge to perform their roles excellently;
4. Bring people together to benefit from the fruits of team play;
5. Leverage the freedom factor;
6. Nurture achievement through measurement and rewards;
7. Base job design decisions on research.

These seven items are deceptively plain and simple-looking in print, but so difficult to implement in reality.

Competing aggressively for talented people means not only hiring the best available people, but paying them what it takes to get and keep them. When I was in Central National's trust department, it was well known that the investment division officers received almost twice the salary that the administrators received; however, the investment officers were also sought by private money managers who offered salaries comparable with what was the going, higher, rate in that industry, not what the bank would normally have paid at the "Work Grade." The only way to keep experienced investment personnel was to throw the normal pay scales out the window.

Offering a vision means more than simply, "We want to be the best in the business." It means having the entire firm deal with what it means to work at Company X; who you are, where you want to go—everything. This is not simply the Chairman's idea. In the first place, he or she may not be able to articulate the vision; in the second place, the Chairman does not have a monopoly on what the firm should be. Offering a vision means clearly enunciating the goals and expectations of the firm, stating what the culture expects from everyone and what it in turn will deliver.

Equipping people with skills and knowledge means a firm-wide, long-term commitment to spending money—seemingly lavishly—on training, both in job-specific skills (for lawyers and accountants, among others, paying for the continuing education courses needed to maintain certification) and in skills that seem to have no direct bearing on the job, but that mean much to customers. Martin (1994) describes a trip he took where he became, in his words, "intangible" to many service-firm employees; this concern mirrors my concerns mentioned below in Chapter 6 and elsewhere (Cahill, 1996). These "nonessential" skills, these skills that have nothing to do with "competence," have nothing to do with getting the work out, but have much to do with customer satisfaction in the long run and thus the long-term profitability of the firm.

Bringing people together to benefit from the results of team play is a relatively new concept in services marketing, but one that has been practiced by the best of the service firms for years. Most people do not seem to work well in isolation, and firms know that. Despite all of the help-wanted advertisements that look for "self-starters," most firms do not want such people; most firms want to build teams. The reasons for this are many: at the very least it helps break the proprietary claims to ownership of certain customers and jobs. Salespeople are notorious for claiming ownership of their customer lists, but they are not alone in feeling this way.

Many years ago when I was a railroad clerk, I worked in an office with a group of very senior clerks, most of whom were well into their sixties. One night one of the men went home and had a nonfatal heart attack. After a couple of weeks, the office started getting phone calls from customers saying that they had not received their bills (which were due to be paid five days after the goods were shipped, by Interstate Commerce Commission regulations). It took a couple of days, but finally management decided to check Atz's desk; they drilled out the lock and found a pile of bills dated to his last day at work. It turned out that Atz had worked as a clerk through the Depression. One of the tricks to getting called back the next day was to squirrel away a little work out of each stack that crossed one's desk and pull a stack of work out just before quitting time, thus showing a backlog. Atz forgot to pull the work out before he went home on the day of his heart attack.

Firms need to instill in their employees the feeling that the work and the customers and the jobs belong to the firm, not to the incumbent–while at the same time promoting a climate in which all employees can feel comfortable that their jobs and pay are not threatened by changes in work flow or structure. This is not an easy task, but it is essential for a firm–particularly a service firm–that practices good internal or external marketing.

This leads directly into leveraging the freedom factor. This is essentially the ability to make mistakes without paying the final penalty of termination. This leveraging factor is probably most frequently discussed in terms of a firm's innovation posture, but the freedom to fail goes deeper than simply during innovation or in innovation teams. This is the freedom to learn, and mistakes are often the best teachers. The adages along these lines have become old saws: "If you give a man a fish, he eats today; if you teach him to fish, he can eat for a lifetime."

As a parent, I often find it difficult to stand back and watch my children make mistakes that I could easily prevent; as a teacher to my children, I know that such a stance on my part is necessary to enable them to become responsible adults. Intervention without their asking for it can often lead to dependence. The same is true with employees. Never turn down an appeal for help, of course, nor allow an employee to do something illegal or dangerous. But one has to give employees enough room to screw things up on their own, so that they can learn how to recover from a mistake.

This posture–again–requires a commitment on management's part to spend money on training, training, and more training. Organization wisdom needs to be passed down from senior employees to junior, both formally and informally. Channels need to be created to facilitate that passing along. And employee turnover needs to be kept to a minimum or, obviously, there is no organizational wisdom and there are no senior employees left who remember anything worthwhile to pass along to the newer employees. If there is only one reason for practicing good internal marketing, this is it: Striving to keep turnover to a minimum will pay large dividends for any firm.

Nurturing achievement through measurement and reward goes beyond offering money and recognition. All too often, recognition and reward systems threaten to become ends in themselves.

> "[The] more we get people to think about the reward they're going to get, the less interest they come to have in whatever they had to do to get the reward. . . . Pay people well, pay them fairly–and then do everything you can to take their minds off of [*sic*] money" (Kohn, 1994:15-16).

Although Kohn's statement seems heretical, particularly in the 1990s, it falls squarely in the Hertzberg school from my MBA days that said that money was not a motivator, but the lack of money was a dismotivator. Recognition programs that monetize recognition probably fall into the same category. A simple public, "Thank you" for a job well done probably does as much as a check.

Basing job design decisions on research is important, and represents another ongoing cost that management simply has to bear. Jobs change over time as customers change and the firm changes and the environment changes. Without a continuous monitoring program, jobs can get to be too big–or too small– for one person to handle and need to be redesigned to bring them into line with the new realities. How frequently? That depends. If one keeps on top of changes in the firm's customers, redesigns probably would happen only as frequently as the environment changes.

An example of this kind of redesign is what happened to the practice of employee-benefit law with the passage of the Employee Retirement Income Security Act (ERISA) by Congress in 1974. Prior to the passage of ERISA, employee benefit law was a rather sleepy practice, with not too much change over the years. Overnight, however, the federal government intervened in a big way: Every employee benefit plan had to be rewritten, almost in its entirety, to conform with the new statute. A law firm with many corporate clients in 1970 may have had a very small group of employee benefit lawyers; by the end of the 1970s, that group would probably have had to double in size, with attendant growth in support personnel, merely to take care of the same number of clients.

Berry and Parasuraman's list (see p. 20) is probably not all-encompassing; their book is now more than four years old and others have added to the list–me included. However, it is a start. Any firm that wants to practice internal marketing could do a lot worse than start at this list.

Chapter 2

What Do We Market?

What do we need to market internally? It seems to me that there are two overriding elements to this questions: First, is there anything which we are marketing externally that we need to make sure that our employees have and use? And second, what messages do we want to convey to our employees about our firm?

OUR OWN GOODS AND SERVICES

Too many firms assume that their employees will buy and use the goods and services that the firm provides without any questions on the employees part. Retail outlets frequently have done a better than average job at getting their employees to use the store in the past by providing employee discounts–frequently substantial–on merchandise. When Saks Fifth Avenue finally opened a store in Cleveland several years ago, it was reported in the press that one of the most attractive parts of its compensation plan was the discount employees would get on their merchandise. As a result, Saks was able to draw many women as salespeople who ordinarily would never have thought about clerking in a store but who were already Saks customers from their trips to New York and elsewhere.

Restaurants have traditionally done a good job of getting their employees to eat at the restaurant by providing free meals as part of the compensation package. When I was in college in Washington, DC, in the middle 1960s, Hot Shoppes (Marriott's restaurant chain) frequently sought casual office labor by posting notices on the job board; they paid only minimum wage (but in cash and for eight hours while really only requiring a bit more than six hours in the office). Also, the work was on Saturday, when the school's meal plan was off and they offered a free lunch worth about $2.00, which reduced a student's out-of-pocket expense for a meal by a like amount. Total compensation was thus not quite as paltry as it seemed at first blush.

How well do firms in other industries stack up? Spottily. Banks have typically given their employees free checking accounts with no balance requirements as well as no-annual-fee charge cards to those who qualify, but this also allows the bank a great deal of oversight as to the employees' spending habits. One of the vice presidents in Central National's trust department advised me when I went to work there to take the paycheck out of the employee account and deposit it elsewhere so that the bank could not monitor my spending. Banks have also typically given employees discounts on loans, sometimes as much as one-half of a percentage point. In these cases, however, there has almost always been a recognition by the banking industry that overall wages paid by the industry have been substandard.

Two better reasons to get the employees to use the goods and services provided by the firm are (1) knowledge that they are the best available, because a firm's competitors offer goods and services that are inferior and (2) that for an employee to be seen using a competitor's product would send a wrong message to the public. This is probably the real reason for the notorious employee-purchase plans offered by the Big Three automobile manufacturers: It would look bad for Ford if there were many Hondas in the plant parking lot. Although this reason can be important for product manufacturers, it is not so important for service providers.

Far more important a consideration is that by using the firm's offerings, by becoming a customer of the firm, an employee gets to see both sides of the transaction. Books and articles frequently advise presidents and vice presidents of sales to try to call the office anonymously to see how "normal" customers are handled, or to try to purchase something over the telephone if applicable. Although this is a good practice, this is not quite what I mean. Employees using the firm's services cannot as a rule be disguised as "normal" customers, nor do they need to be. Even if everyone working on their transactions knows that they are employees and thus give better treatment, the employee will see the firm and its offerings in a new light–as a user. Rules and procedures that seem perfectly sensible to the employee as an employee may seem terribly onerous to the employee as a user of the service. Although the benefits of this new insight are difficult to quantify–or prove, for that matter–I believe that they do exist.

A subsidiary benefit to the firm may be enhanced revenue and/or reduced costs or better utilization of personnel. One of the basic problems of having one's employees use the firm's services is on what basis to allow them access to those services. A bank may, in fact, restrict employee access to tellers to specific, nonrush times. This will reduce the lines for "normal" customers at lunchtime and distribute the tellers' useful time better–they will not be standing around with no transactions from opening until 11:30 a.m. Allowing such nonpeak access can permit even discounted business to be done profitably. However, employee access must be carefully monitored, not only to prevent negative impact on direct profitability, but also to avoid upsetting the paying customers. I recently flew from Cleveland to Oregon; all of the flights were full, but the airline was deadheading several employees who got seats ahead of paying passengers. Although there may be good institutional reasons for such a procedure–employees needed in another city to handle planes, employees returning to base from assignment elsewhere, etc.–the fact that these employees were deadheading in uniform made them quite conspicuous and royally upset more than one passenger. In an era when airlines compete so vigorously to get repeat business, several businesspeople around me made severely negative comments about the practice and how it would impact upon their airline choice the next time they flew.

This example is one reason why I commented negatively in Chapter 1 on the reviewer's definition of internal marketing as "good human resources management with a view to satisfying external customers." Here is an example where "good human resources management" comes into conflict with "satisfying external customers." Where does the firm go, which horn of the dilemma does it choose to grasp? Employee morale? Goodness knows that if I were an employee deadheading back from Paris to my base in Denver because I got left in Paris because of equipment needs, I would want to get the first plane back. However, as an external customer, that employee had better not keep me from getting the seat that I paid for and told people at my destination that I would be using. This leads indirectly to Cahill's First Law of Marketing: Take Care of the Customers and Profits Will Take Care of Themselves. What is its applicability here? The airline should buy the deadheading employee a ticket on a competing airline to prevent any paying customers from being inconvenienced. This action would not only satisfy the passengers, who would get the seats they had bought and paid for, but would also satisfy the employee, who would get where he or she was going almost as quickly as if deadheading.

Buying that deadheading employee a seat on a competing airline would also achieve another, almost contradictory, goal of the recent services marketing literature: getting employees to know the competition. It may seem difficult to get employees to know the competition intimately if they are constantly using the firm's offerings, and it probably is. Nevertheless, some sort of formal, conscious attention to one's competitors will frequently pay enormous dividends. This program need not be a full-blown "benchmarking" study such as some TQM (Total Quality Marketing) people advocate; one simply needs to know what the competition is up to, even in the little things. As an example of how small changes may please customers (and therefore need to be considered), look at the change in many airlines' policies about soft drinks. A couple of years ago it was almost unheard of to be offered the full can (just a glass was considered enough); now, more and more airlines are giving passengers the choice. Cost to the airline? It cannot be very much. Are customers pleased at the change? I know that I am, and I doubt that I am alone.

VISION MESSAGES

Beyond marketing goods and services, what else should be included in an internal marketing program? First in importance must be formal messages from management to the employees about what many authors call the "vision" of the firm: who the firm is, what it does, why and how it does it, who its customers are. These messages are crucial to the smooth operation of any firm, whether manufacturing or service, but probably more necessary in a service firm because no one can point to a physical product and say "That's us" or, conversely, "That's *not* us."

Vision messages are very important. One of the most important aspects of leadership has always been to impart a vision of the enterprise to the rest of the enterprise. In the 1990s we no longer concede to the leaders the right to be the only people who can have a vision for the enterprise. Part of the movement in management which bears many names (job enrichment, employee empowerment, etc.) has been the destruction of what organization scholars call the "elite viewpoint." Others in the organization can have a vision and routinely *do* have a vision of the organization. Since leaders are rarely on the front line with customers, it often is the front-line employee's vision of the organization, and not the leader's that colors the experience the *customer* will have with that organization.

Therefore, it is incumbent upon the leader to make sure that the leader's vision is generally shared by the employees. Some specific techniques to help that process are presented in Chapter 4. What I want to talk about now are a couple of messages that need to be sent if the service firm is to do well.

The first of these messages is almost a self-congratulatory "We are great!" No employee, no firm, wants to be thought of as mediocre–not by others and not by oneself. Pats on the back for a job well done, recognition for service to customers above and beyond the call of duty (as Federal Express does so well) help to permeate the organization with this sense of greatness. The leadership needs to spell out exactly how it defines "Greatness" and then admit it when it happens–and admit failure when it does not. Wilson Brown, Central National's president in the early 1980s, said at an officers' meeting that banking was an easy business: "It consists of gathering lots of little deposits in a retail fashion and making big loans wholesale." The spread between retail and wholesale (a reverse spread in this case) is the bank's profit margin and can be fairly accurately forecast if one does not attempt to go too far into the future with the forecast. Central failed abysmally because someone forgot Brown's statement of what the banking business consisted of–and paid for the failure with its life. Prior to its demise, however, Central *was* great–a great bank to work for and great for its customers. Not too big that it had lost its human touch, but big enough to accommodate almost any request placed upon it by customers from its target market.

DO IT RIGHT THE FIRST TIME

A more important message, certainly for service firms, is "Do it right the first time," or, as Berry and Parasuraman (1991) bluntly state, "Do it very right the second time." This message is essentially one that says "Our people are competent." This is the message that all successful service firms provide for their external markets. This message is crucial for internal marketing to send to employees–"Incompetence will not be tolerated." This is not to say that mistakes will not be tolerated; not only are service employees human and thus subject to error, but for innovation to occur, people have to experiment and experiments lead to mistakes and failure.

One way to limit mistakes is, of course, to limit human involvement in the service process, to "industrialize" the service in the same way that industrialization and automation of manufacturing in the past two centuries has made it possible to have "Six Sigma Quality." Theodore Levitt (1974), in his article titled "The Industrialization of Service," states that there are three methods to industrialize services: hard, soft (operating procedures), and hybrid technologies. I have been associated with several attempts to industrialize services, primarily through hybrid technologies; few I have been associated with or know about have been successful. (See Cahill, 1990, 1993; Cahill and Warshawsky, 1993, 1995; Cahill, Warshawsky, and Thach, 1994, for the details about these attempts at industrializing services.)

What went wrong with these attempts at automation? The most important factor has to be cost. Automation efforts at least imply a capital-budgeting arrangement, whereby up-front costs are recouped (one hopes at a profit) by reducing expenses over time; this is a straightforward concept that I teach in undergraduate Financial Management classes. The problem is that it is often easy to pinpoint the costs involved, but frequently very difficult to identify the expense reductions with any certainty, either as to occurrence or amount. A second factor is the innovative firm's frequent inability to let go of a potential idea even when it becomes relatively clear that it will not work the way it was supposed to, or come in on time, or on budget.

Innovation and competence rarely go hand in hand in the short run. Innovation, by definition, means new things; innovation in services means doing things a new way. Competence, whether for a clerk filling out routing slips, a lawyer drafting a will to take new tax laws into consideration, or for a skater in landing her jumps consists of long hours of practice. Repetition, not innovation. We all marvel at a quarterback's ability to find an open receiver downfield (say, his tertiary receiver) and get the ball to him; in fact, television commentators often talk about "peripheral vision," "God-given talent" or some other old saw. What gives the quarterback-receiver team the ability to take a broken play–the tertiary opening–is long hours together on the practice field throwing and catching and learning what each will do in a given situation. Take that same quarterback and give him the most physically gifted receiver, with no opportunity to practice beyond a week or two of running the basic plays, and watch the football drop uncaught time and time again.

Innovation does that to people outside the realm of athletics as well. When the service design changes, the routine is broken, and people are apt to make mistakes; recognizing that this is the case, many people slow down while they are learning the new, making it difficult to meet service temporal objectives even if the work done is error free. A firm needs to be careful about the number of service innovations it introduces at any time, allowing employees and customers to become comfortable with each innovation before introducing another.

For a service firm to be successful, it must consistently provide services that at least meet the expectations of its clientele. As we shall see, this matching requires a substantial amount of effort and organization. And, if the firm is unable to match expectations with performance, all its other marketing efforts–even the accurate performance of the task for which it has been retained–will go for naught. In fact, the lack of matching of expectations and performance may be the most damaging aspect of a firm's attempt to garner repeat business.

MANAGING CLIENT EXPECTATIONS

The matching of expectations with performance actually consists of two separate assignments: (1) managing the client's expectations to a level the organization can meet on a sustained basis (Davidow and Uttal, 1989); and (2) communication to the service providers within the organization as to the levels of service that they are expected to provide. The successful organization will accomplish *both* of these objectives. Raising client expectations and failing to deliver service to that level of quality is a sure path to disaster, while defining excellent service levels without letting the clients know about it is totally ineffective as well as running costs up without a concomitant ability to raise fees.

The key is to identify techniques which will, at the same time, define client expectations and crystallize performance levels. Since the marketing of services is a comparatively new field, there is little information available on service marketing techniques. We can gain some insight by examining how sellers of tangible goods approach these same questions. At first blush, the task of managing expectations for consumers of tangible products seems easy. The consumer can see, feel, and often test the product before purchasing it. As is often the case in human behavior, what seems simple on the surface is actually highly complex. A new field of marketing, known as Symbolic Consumer Behavior, has arisen to address the aspects of what makes consumers tick at depths below the surface.

In a seminal article on the subject, Elizabeth Hirschman states that two people hearing the same advertisement or seeing the same hamburger may call into consciousness totally different associations. The internal meaning may be different for each person, even though the external stimulus may be the same for both. "It is possible that we are not all perceiving the same 'bundle of attributes' when we observe a hamburger. Further . . . the attributes associated with the hamburger may not even contribute the bulk of its meaning to the consumer" (Hirschman, 1980). According to the theory of Symbolic Consumer Behavior, the physical attributes of a product have relatively little meaning to the consumer compared to its intangible aspects–packaging, advertising messages, where it is sold, and the reputation of the seller and manufacturer.

The sellers of tangible products thus face much the same problem as the sellers of services, namely how to manage customer expectations with respect to intangibles. A widely used approach to this problem is the product warranty or guarantee. Many retailers have long based their principal marketing efforts upon their warranty policies. Craftsman tools are sold by Sears, Roebuck with a lifetime replacement warranty. If the tool *ever* breaks, Sears replaces it. Period. Many customers will buy no other brand of tools because they enjoy the peace of mind and assurance of quality conveyed by that Craftsman warranty.

Product warranties and guarantees are old hat in product sales. While less common in service businesses, they form the basis for some success stories. Federal Express is noted for its promise, "when it absolutely, positively has to be there overnight." But what does this guarantee really encompass? If Federal Express fails to deliver on time, it simply refunds the fee for the botched delivery. To the customer, however, the promise conveys a strong assurance of quality service and a caring attitude about the customer's problems. H & R Block advertises that if it makes a mistake on your tax return that causes you to pay more tax, it will pay the interest and penalties due on that return. While Block knows that the vast majority of the returns it prepares are so simple that the probability of error is slight, the customers receive assurance that Block cares about what happens to them, and the firm is willing to stand behind its work.

Both Block and Fed Ex pay on them from time to time. The guarantees serve the purpose of reassuring clients that the failure of the organization to perform up to standard will not result in cost to them. And, as important, the guarantees communicate to employees in the organization (1) what performance standards will be; (2) that substandard performance bears an organizational price; and (3) that repeated lapses from standard performance cannot be tolerated.

UNCONDITIONAL GUARANTEES

An even more compelling case history is discussed in Christopher Hart's article on unconditional service guarantees (Hart, 1988). "Bugs" Burger Bug Killers (BBBK; the company is now named Prism), a Miami-based exterminator whose clients consist principally of restaurants and hotels, has such an unconditional guarantee. While most exterminators claim they will reduce pests to some defined acceptable level, BBBK promises to eliminate them entirely. Its Service Guarantee as discussed by Hart (it is somewhat different today):

1. The customer makes no payment until all pests have been eliminated.
2. If BBBK fails to eliminate all pests, it will refund up to 12 months of fees and will pay for another exterminator for a year.
3. If a guest spots a pest, BBBK will pay for that guest's meal or room, send the guest a letter of apology, and pay for a future meal or room for that guest.
4. If the premises are closed due to roaches or rodents, BBBK will pay all fines and lost profits, plus $5,000.

In short, BBBK says if they do not satisfy their clients 100 percent, they do not want their money. Period. Is the BBBK guarantee a success? The firm operates all over the United States, charges fees up to ten times those of its competitors, and has a disproportionately high market share in the areas in which it operates. In 1986, it paid guarantee claims of $120,000 on sales of $33 million, or about one-third of one percent (Hart, 1988).

An unconditional service guarantee helps market professional services by eliminating what computer people call the "FUD Factor"–Fear, Uncertainty, and Doubt. Services cannot be test driven before they are bought, so there is often a high risk factor in choosing a service provider. Many services can be used only once and not returned after use. Once a will is written by the lawyer, the service has been used up. A consultant's recommendations that do not work cannot be returned to the consultant. Most people cannot imagine a higher risk than an Internal Revenue Service audit caused by a "bad" tax return, or the chaos in one's estate caused by a "bad" will. An unconditional guarantee, bolstered by a reputation for delivering high quality service, will go far in alleviating the FUD Factor.

What makes a good guarantee? It is unconditional, easy to understand and communicate, meaningful, easy to invoke, and easy and quick to collect on (Hart, 1988). One must avoid provisions that vitiate the effect of the guarantee. A client of mine once established a 30-day guarantee program. It required the customer to come to a hard-to-find office during specified hours, fill out a lengthy form, and accept a check in payment, whether the customer had tendered cash or a check. The manager of the operation delighted in keeping guarantee payments at absurdly low levels, thus eliminating the meaningfulness of the guarantee to the customers–and to the organization.

Guarantees can do three things for the organization, if properly put into place. First, as already mentioned, they can serve notice to the service providers in the organization that there are standards of service that must be met. And there is little point in setting these standards too low; the customers will soon be aware that, although the firm meets its standards, say 95 percent of the time, its standards do not mean much in the real world. Standards should be attainable, but should require consistently good levels of performance.

Second, unconditional service guarantees can focus the attention of the organization on areas of its business where service–in the everyday definition of the word–should have a major impact. Often, executives claim that they could not possibly offer an unconditional guarantee. In fact, in the issue of *Harvard Business Review* after Hart's article appeared, there were several letters to the editor about why the concept would not work. Bruce Henderson (Professor of Management at Vanderbilt University), after quoting a personal story about how Sears, Roebuck's unconditional guarantee on batteries made him a loyal Sears customer for years, states that such a guarantee would "appear to be an invitation to unlimited liability in an era of runaway litigation and megabuck damage awards." Creating an unconditional service guarantee "requires an equation that optimizes the relationship between cost, benefits, feasibility, and sustainability of and shifts in competitive advantage" (Henderson, 1988:172). Henderson seems to take the same dismal view of customers that many businesspeople have. Every time I discuss the concept of unconditional service guarantees with clients, I hear the lament, "It'll never work; everyone will claim against the guarantee." Yet remember the Burger Bug Killer example above: $120,000 in claims against $33 million in sales—hardly "everyone." Burger cannot be unique. Some years ago, Piedmont Airlines (now a part of USAir) gave their front-line personnel the authority to write free tickets for lost luggage and ticketing snafus; the finance people claimed that the airline would be bankrupt in short order. According to Donald Shanks, Vice President of Customer Relations, the dollar amount of free tickets *declined* when people were *immediately* offered the ticket as opposed to having to wait for satisfaction (Shanks, 1985). In fact, most customers will be extremely reluctant to press a claim beyond a minimal reasonable amount when faced with immediate (this is the key) satisfaction for that claim.

Third, guarantees can provide a firm with marketing impact, particularly if the firm is the first in a market to offer such a guarantee. The odds of gaining powerful marketing impact from such a guarantee are in one's favor when one or more of the following conditions are met (Hart, 1988):

1. The price of the service is high. Although most professional-service providers' hourly rates are not necessarily high

by objective standards, to many clients the idea of charging for time by the hour makes the bills *seem* high.

2. The customer's ego is on the line. An individual I know had to file an amended tax return less than two weeks after the original return had been filed because of the failure of his accountant to include $250,000 in rental income on the personal return that the same accountant had deducted as rental expense on the corporate return.
3. The customer's expertise with the service is low. Most people hire professionals either because they cannot or will not perform those services themselves.
4. The negative consequences of service failure are high.
5. The industry has a bad image for service quality.
6. The company depends on frequent rebuys from the same customers. Most service professionals depend upon ongoing relationships with the same clients for success, even if not strictly defined "rebuys."
7. The company's business is affected deeply by word of mouth. The statistics of complaining behavior on the part of dissatisfied customers have entered business folklore. In one study on durable goods, 54 percent of the dissatisfied buyers said they would not purchase again and 45 percent said that they warned a friend against purchase (Hawkins, Best, and Coney, 1986). Study after study has indicated that many times more people go away mad (and tell their friends) than complain to the company. A customer will tell many more people about a bad experience than about a good experience. Virtually *any* business can be deeply affected by word of mouth.

The purpose of an unconditional service guarantee is not to lower consumer complaints and costs associated with those complaints. The entire objective is to *increase* complaints. A study of 540 consumers of grocery products recalled 1,307 separate unsatisfactory purchases; 25 percent of these purchases resulted in brand switching, and 19 percent caused the shopper to stop buying the product. However, only 3 percent complained to the manufacturer, 5 percent complained to the retailer, and 35 percent returned the item. . . . *58 percent did nothing!* The manufacturer has no way of improving these grocery items if no one tells the firm why the product is unsatisfactory (Hawkins, Best, and Coney, 1986:693). This is why the guarantee must be unconditional, meaningful to the customer, and easy to apply for. The more obstacles that are thrown in the way of the complaining customer, the more likely that customer is to remain silent–and that is the worst thing that can happen to a business. Lost business is hard to replace; it is doubly hard when one has no idea why it is lost, and at least doubly hard again when one does not even know it is lost for some time afterward. No one enjoys listening to client complaints, but we must consider John Guaspari's "3 R's of Quality" (Guaspari, 1988):

- Realize that the customer has all the votes when it comes to quality;
- Remember that the customer has all the votes when it comes to quality;
- Recognize that the fact that the customer has all the votes when it comes to quality is as it should be.

And quality is what an unconditional service guarantee is all about. In a preliminary study comparing responses to dissatisfaction with products and services, the authors state that despite a more knowledgeable and "upscale" sample than the general population, there was "no clear consensus [by respondents] on what action to take in response to unsatisfactory experiences," particularly "once a direct appeal to the service provider is unsuccessful" (Levy and Surprenant, 1982).

How to implement an unconditional service guarantee? The five steps are as follows:

1. Senior management must decide to pay the price, both monetary and psychic, for installing such a guarantee. The entire organization must be re-focused toward total commitment to the concept, in a complete transformation of the firm's culture. Without this commitment, any "tinkering" with an unconditional guarantee will only raise the firm's cost of meeting the guarantee without any of the financial benefits that should accrue, as discussed above.

2. The firm must conduct market research, including surveys, focus groups, interviews with existing clients, interviews with former clients, etc., to determine several things. First, what is clients' perception of the firm now? Is it seen as responsive and a quality service provider? Second, what lines of business do clients see as important? Is the firm providing these lines? Do clients know this? It is at this point that offering a "limited" unconditional service guarantee first becomes possible. If it seems impossible to guarantee everything about all the lines of service that the firm provides, a limited guarantee for limited lines is better than nothing and may point the way for the firm to expand the guarantee at a later date.

3. The firm must train its employees. This is not limited to training to raise technical competence; clients have a right to expect competence from service providers and firms have an incentive (lower incidence of error-caused claims) to insist on competence from their employees. Henderson is correct about the litigious nature of clients. However, given the fact that there is at least an implicit guarantee on professional services imposed by the courts if not by the provider, it would behoove the service provider to train its employees to inculcate a sensitivity to the needs of being on the front line for client service. This is a new role for service providers, but it is a crucial role. The service provider becomes critical in delivering client satisfaction. For products, the reliance on retailers is overwhelming–almost 90 percent of initial responses to dissatisfaction involved returning

the product to the retailer. This dominance is not so clear-cut for services; however, "complaining to the provider is still the most popular initial action" (Levy and Surprenant, 1982). When we remember the statement by Levy and Surprenant mentioned above–that those surveyed did not have a clear sense of how to appeal to the service providers–the importance of this training becomes indisputable.

4. The firm must commit to stay close to what the clients want. Forever. This will necessitate establishing quantitative and qualitative measures to ensure that the new outlook of the firm is translated into procedures that allow the firm to continue the unconditional guarantee (*Close to the Customer,* 1987). Although this is similar to the statement in item 1 above, it is not identical. This is where the essence of being a "client-centered" or "market-driven" firm enters; one's clients will henceforth dictate what the firm provides, not the firm itself.

5. The firm must determine what to guarantee. The answer: Whatever it is in the service provided that clients find to be most important. To BBBK's customers, it is the complete freedom from vermin. To an accountant's clients, it might be "no penalties from IRS audits." To a consultant's clients it might be timely delivery of all reports. By warranting that which the client deems crucial, the service provider will perforce be aiming the quality effort in the correct direction. Again, this seems similar to item 3 above, but it has a different focus. The focus here is again on the *client's* desires. It is not on "what can the firm do" but, rather, on "what do the clients need."

In summary, we have seen how a service organization can, through the careful design and communication of a service guarantee, manage the expectations of its clients to a level that the firm can consistently meet, and also convey to the employees a clear sense of purpose and expected levels of performance. To the extent that such a guarantee is limited by various conditions, it loses much of its effectiveness for such purposes. An unconditional service guarantee packs the greatest punch, and delivers the most forceful message to clients and employees alike. And, while the cost of an unconditional guarantee may well exceed that of a conditional guarantee, the cost would fade into insignificance when compared with the resulting gains in revenues and profitability. Remember BBBK's $120,000 expense on $33 million of revenue. It is critical to the successful implementation of a guarantee program that management be fully committed to bear the costs in terms of market research, employee training, and warranty claims themselves. The unconditional service guarantee offers a unique opportunity to create a successful service organization to the firms that have the foresight to implement them.

HIRING AND TRAINING PEOPLE

Service firms–particularly professional service firms–seem to be more team-based than manufacturing firms. It probably is in the nature of the service offering and delivery process. The Central National Bank corporate trust division, when I was there, consisted of five officers, three administrative assistants, and two secretaries; we handled several hundred accounts, ranging in size from a few thousand dollars to hundreds of millions, from one employee to thousands. We handled pension plans, profit-sharing and other defined-contribution plans, IRAs, bond indentures and other miscellaneous accounts. Each account was assigned to an officer and he (all the officers were male in those days) and his administrative assistant (whom he shared with another officer) handled all the work. Nevertheless, due to vacations, being out on business calls, and other vagaries, it never failed that at least once a week there was a crisis in someone's account when he was gone. We all pitched in without demur–officers and administrative assistants alike–knowing that next time it might be one of our accounts that blew up, and the account belonged to corporate trust.

That good bunch of people was not hired, trained, nor given incentives to act like that; Central was just lucky, although the atmosphere that engendered this kind of a response was deliberately nurtured by the head of the trust department. The head of the corporate trust division did not hold staff meetings to rouse the troops (he so hated meetings of any kind that he would stay in the few staff meetings he called only long enough to go down the items he had put on the agenda and would leave if anyone talked too long); we did not have a song or slogan or lapel pin; we never went on retreat together, or out to lunch as a unit, or performed any of the actions that are so often mentioned in the team-building literature. Yet we were a team: We thought of ourselves as a team and we acted as a team. Much of the rest of the trust department laughed at us for our attitude, but we did not care.

How does a firm go about hiring people who will work with the rest of the people in the organization? Verrrrry carefully, to paraphrase Arte Johnson of *Laugh-In.* Obviously, competence enters into the equation; it must be assumed. This, of course, does *not* mean not to hire rookies, or else they would never get their first job, nor would anyone ever be able to change careers. It is possible to transfer competence from one job to another, even if the technical skills are not directly transferable. But there must be more than competence. Customer orientation is important, probably more important than technical competence.

I was hired away from Central National Bank by Society National in 1982 on the recommendation of the head of the employee benefit section of Society's outside law firm with whom I had worked from time to time on some complicated employee benefit plans; I had obviously impressed him with my technical competence and willingness to get things done for the customer. In fact, my first exposure to Russ happened after I had been at Central only a couple of months when he needed to have some documents signed "Right Now" and no one at Central had had time to read them. I told him that what he wanted was impossible, but that if he sent them over, I would get on it immediately. He sent the papers over, calmed down, and called my boss to tell him how impressed he had been by my adherence to procedure in the face of pressure. My boss exploded and told me that the next time someone from a major law firm wanted something signed, that I should just sign it, whereupon Russ told Bob that he was wrong, that the trustee had "damn well better read what we draft."

Anyhow, I went to Society with several years' business experience and trust experience all aimed at taking care of the customers first and the organization I worked for second. I did not last terribly long at Society because their priorities in the trust department were reversed. Society refused to handle certain types of trusts because they were too complicated, or they involved exposing the department to unusual transactions. One type of trust that I was very familiar with and had sold with some degree of success at Central was leveraged leases–very complex corporate deals that often required the trustee to own assets in various states. Central had insisted that an individual be co-trustee to own assets in those states where statutes made life difficult for foreign banks. Society refused to own real estate in any state other than Ohio and would not take any such real estate into any trust, personal or otherwise. Often their first response was "No, we don't do that." This is hardly a stance designed to endear a firm to its customers.

New employees need to be screened to determine the extent of their customer orientation and, unfortunately, I know of no test or other instrument that will do the screening. Reviewing resumes will not do the job, either. But long talks (not "interviews") with the candidates can help, as can role playing. Since it is one of the theses of this book that employees' customer orientation is crucial to a service firm's success, and that any well-designed internal marketing program must be drawn to foster that orientation, this is not a meaningless exercise. Too often, "interviews" are conducted simply to determine whether an individual will "fit" in the firm's "culture," i.e., does the candidate dress right and talk right and play the right games. Not only does such an interviewing strategy tend to reduce the diversity of the work force, it does not get at the important question of customer orientation at all.

Employee promotion needs another look as well. Too frequently, organizations promote people based upon their technical competence and performance at their position, rather than on the basis of the needs of the prospective position–thus the sales manager who was promoted because he was the most productive salesperson in the firm. This of course makes the job of the newly promoted manager doubly difficult, for the most productive salesperson is no longer in place selling. Not to mention that the new manager has probably never managed anything more difficult than his or her own calendar and has no real idea how to begin. There are lots of courses around for the "Newly Promoted Sales Manager," but by the time the salesperson has been promoted it is already too late to start the education process.

Worse, this kind of promotion practice, which is certainly *not* the exclusive purview of sales forces, focuses upon the technical demands of the positions reporting to it, of the department in which it resides, rather than on what the customers want and need, whether those customers are internal or external. In the organization that I espouse throughout this book–one in which technical competence is assumed–employees would be promoted based largely upon how well they meet customer demands associated with their current job and the department in which they currently work. This is probably the best guide to how customer-oriented they will be in any new position. And in the firm which truly implements a good internal marketing program, customer orientation is one of the few things that matters.

One of the keys to handling employees in firms that do internal marketing is to lavish attention and recognition on them. Sales organizations have always known this. Recognition in front of employees' peers is a powerful motivator; incentive programs with lots of publicity can do wonders to get even disgruntled employees–the always-present grumblers, clock-watchers, and latrine-lawyers–to do what management wants them to do. But this recognition and any incentives must be genuine and attainable or the incentive will backfire quickly.

One of my favorite stories about recognition being more important than monetary reward (once the employees' basic needs are taken care of, of course) goes back to my days in the credit department at Medusa Cement–right after I had earned my MBA. Medusa in those days had seven sales divisions. Each year, the salesmen–in those days all men and all on salary–competed on tonnage shipped (raw, with no factoring for profitability among several different products, nor deduction for tonnage shipped but not paid for, etc.–not a good system). The salesman from each division who sold the most tonnage was taken, along with his wife, to a sales department dinner at a hotel in Cleveland (the headquarters) and given a "Medusa Coat." The coat was Medusa blue; the only way to describe Medusa blue is to say that it was bright and would foil any attempt to wear with any other article of clothing. One of the salesmen who was particularly friendly to me commented that he was coming up to Cleveland for the ceremony and wanted to meet me. I congratulated him and mentioned that the jacket must be a nice one, since he took such obvious pride in winning it.

"Nah," was his response. "I already have four of the damned things in my closet that I can't wear anywhere. I just like to wear them to our sales division meetings and rub everyone else's noses in the fact that I'm the best damned salesman in the division"–clearly not the response of a "team player," but one that must be reckoned with.

Recognition–more than the monetary value of the goodies given as the token of that recognition–is key here. It undoubtedly does far more good for the organization and its employees to have a company dinner and give out an inexpensive plaque or desktop item for everyone to see on a frequent basis and remember why the individual was given the item than to spend a similar (or greater) amount of money on a catalogue system. Too often, the catalogue incentive systems have the employees buy items for themselves or their house; if the employees need to be put on a commission basis, by all means do so–and pay frequently and in cash. If one is trying to give incentives for performance, patting the employees on the back–and gently reminding the other employees about the pats on the back–works better.

Recognition is a crucial item. Company newsletters are old hat. If you do not have one, start one; if you have one, spruce it up. It is not just management's organ for delivering overinflated pronouncements about the company's accomplishments; it is a great place for employees to brag about themselves and their accomplishments or the company to brag about its employees. Service pins are another idea that is trite–but not stale.

A client of mine started a service-pin program about six years ago. The firm has a Christmas party at headquarters where the Chairman hands out bonus checks to everyone–and then goes to many of the subsidiary operations over the next week to do the same. In 1989 he also handed out service pins–and put his Founder's Pin on first, after a short speech explaining what it was. For the next three years, most of the employees wore their lapel pins most of the time, very proudly. Unfortunately, there was insufficient follow-through by the client to continue the program, but I saw firsthand how such a little item as a lapel pin can increase employee pride. And an employee who is proud to be associated with your firm is already easier to encourage to do things the way you want them done than one who is not proud to be your employee, even if he or she is not actually ashamed.

All of these activities must be genuine and perceived as such by your employees. A large bank in Cleveland recently gave all of their employees T-shirts to identify themselves because they were each going to spend four hours doing "community work."

Everyone from the president on down was required to wear the T-shirt to work one day so that everyone in town could see them; the next week they were to perform their community service, wearing the shirt for identification. Of course the newspapers and television stations shot pictures and did stories of senior executives doing community service so the bank got an awful lot of publicity out of this activity. Was this the goal of the activity from the beginning? One may raise the question; after all, the bank's name was quite prominent on the shirt–and it showed up easily even in relatively small newspaper pictures.

Large organizations have a credibility problem in late-twentieth century America, largely as a result of years of actions that do not square with the public pronouncements of managers of those organizations. I have worked as a unionized railroad clerk while I went to college, a low-level officer at a bank, and a very low-level instructional employee at a large university; always, at these levels, the employees were cynical about the motives of the organizations that employed them. This cynicism was frequently corrosive of motivation and performance, not only of the cynical employee but also of the rest of the employees around them. I spent three summers as a summer relief clerk for a railroad's billing office–a job of unrelenting (if air-conditioned) boredom, cyclicality, and mind-numbing speed needed to handle 5,000 bills per day. One day, all of the chief clerks and managers (about ten people) were closeted in a room for the entire day to discuss whether the transmittal slips which went with each packet of billing data should be done in blue ink and red carbon paper or red ink and blue carbon paper. The decision was ultimately made to use red pens and blue carbon paper "or else the pens would all walk out of the office." This was when stick pens cost about a dime, retail. I inadvertently took several red pens, because I used to tuck them behind my ear and forget about them. This kind of waste of managerial and supervisory resources made the manager of this office of over a hundred clerks a laughing stock. Genuine motivation comes from genuine concern.

Chapter 3

To Whom Do We Market Internally?

Segmentation–the dividing of a total market into its component parts by some scheme–is not new. It has been around as a marketing tool for so long that a countervailing wisdom developed almost 20 years ago advocating that for some products and services the provider should not segment because segmentation was too expensive to be worth doing. As a general rule, however, marketers in the last generation have segmented their markets more often than not. In fact, at times they have probably over-segmented their markets. We are now inundated with dozens of varieties of various products that, until recently, would probably not have existed or–if they did exist–would have been marketed under different brands. There has been a literature developed in the last few years bitterly condemning what are called "brand extensions"–where a brand name is used on products that are different from the original: Coke begets Diet Coke begets Caffeine Free Diet Coke begets Cherry Coke, etc. In the process, the original product can get lost and the "franchise" built up over the years can be diluted. In the case of "Miller Lite," it is often claimed that the success of this extension all but destroyed the original "Miller High Life." (See Ries and Trout [1986] for the most vitriolic example of this kind of thinking.)

SEGMENTATION SCHEMES AND STRATEGIES

When faced with the concept of segmentation for the first time, undergraduate students usually decide that the basis for segmentation is by differences: what makes Group A different from Group B. However, what is more important–certainly for a pragmatic marketing application–is similarities: What makes the members of Group A more like each other than like the members of Group B. This allows us, using one or more of several statistical techniques, to cluster the respondents into groups, and then target our appeals to the members of a particular group, creating what are termed "target markets."

A "target market" is, at its most basic, simply the market or submarket (such as segment) at which the firm aims its marketing message(s). There is nothing inherent in the concept of target marketing that requires a firm to segment, or, having segmented, to develop multiple product offerings or marketing messages. It simply means that a group of customers has been identified for whom the offering should be "right" and to whom the firm will direct the majority of its marketing time, resources, and attention, with the rationale that it is better to use a rifle than a shotgun to get results. (This rationale possibly should be reconsidered; in the infamous Gunfight at the OK Corral it was Doc Holliday using a shotgun who killed people, not the Earps using pistols.) Nevertheless, it seems usual that when firms target market, they do so for multiple targets within a broader market.

The current state of "interactive technology" has caught the eye of a few marketing thinkers in the past couple of years. Peppers and Rogers (1993) have posited what they call "one-to-one" marketing, where the vendor will be in direct contact (and vice versa) with each potential buyer, seeking what they call "share of customer" rather than "market share." Although their book is a bit evangelical and does not consider the real difficulties many (if not most) marketers will have in establishing and using such a system, it has real applicability in internal marketing situations; therefore, will refer to it in Chapter 4.

The argument arises at this point: "What does any of this matter? We are talking about internal marketing and what my employees have in common is that they work for XYZ, Inc. And, by God, they'll listen to messages from me because I'm the boss." My first question would be to ask the individual what planet he had been living on for the past 20 years; employees may have been like that in some Arcadian past (I doubt it–I've been working since 1966 and I have not seen anything to resemble the above statement), but they are not like that now. I am reminded of an incident early in my MBA classes in the mid-1970s. We were discussing some point in a labor class when one of the students thundered out, "If they don't like it, they can punch in or picket." The class erupted with laughter, but the point was taken; I doubt that many would utter that line today. Employees are not all alike; different approaches will work with different people; different departments, facilities, and levels will have different needs. All of these differences need to be taken into consideration, dealing with what Foxall and Goldsmith (1994) label as "Consumers in Context"–or, more properly in this case I suppose, employees in context. An internal marketing program will probably have to be targeted and segmented, just like an external marketing program would be. So how do we actually do the segmentation? There are four basic approaches to segmenting populations, although combinations of two or more do exist. These approaches are geographic, demographic, psychographic, and behavioral methods.

Geographic segmentation schemes are probably the oldest segmentation method of all. At root, it assumes that people have needs because of where they live that are different from those of people who live elsewhere. The old saw about selling refrigerators to the Eskimos, is a recognition of geographic segmentation's underlying principle. Remembering that we are seeking to group like with like, so geographic segmentation has a lot to recommend it, particularly in internal marketing situations. People at the same facility will possibly have needs that are more like one another's than the needs of employees at another facility across the country or in another country. Large, multi-office law firms, those with offices in several states (and now, foreign countries as well) may find that they need to approach many of their internal marketing needs on a geographic basis, or partly geographically, as different jurisdictions have different licensing requirements and different approaches to achieving the same ends. When their clients also span different states and different countries, geographical segmentation makes sense.

Demographic segmentation is the second-oldest consumer segmentation scheme. This is the old Bureau-of-the-Census approach: race, creed, sex, national origin, age, ability, and income. Although this has many benefits for product and services segmenting, as an approach for segmenting internal markets I think it leaves something to be desired–except for specific needs. Offering retirement planning to employees under 30 probably is a waste of time, for example. Otherwise, since most of the demographic categories also fall into the areas where firms have to be careful about discrimination under various federal statutes, demographic segmentation by itself probably creates more problems than it solves.

Psychographic segmentation has been around for more than a generation (Demby, 1989); it uses life-style, social class, values, attitudes, and other psychological attributes–often overlaid atop some basic demographic data–to create multiple segments. Probably the most famous psychographic segmentation scheme was VALS (Values and Life Styles, produced by SRI, formerly Stanford Research International), which was not truly a psychographic segmentation scheme at all (more about VALS later in this chapter). At its heart, psychographics says that what people think and believe, the values they hold, and how they live and spend their money allows researchers a window into their behavior. This has led to massive literature on whether attitudes lead to behavior or not; whether VALS or the List of Values (LOV), developed by Lynn Kahle and others (Kahle, 1983) works better; whether values change or not; and on and on. (See Appendix 2 for a technical discussion of marketing typologies in general and VALS and LOV in particular.)

Psychographic segmentation schemes have been very popular in the academic press as well as the marketplace. Frequently reviled by nonusers as "flashy and unnecessary," one must be reminded from time to time about the purpose behind the use of psychographics. ". . . [These] profiles were not designed to take the place of all other research tools. . . . Psychographic profiles should augment a total research and analysis package . . ." (Wasson, 1987). Wells (1975) made the same point 20 years ago in what was probably the first review essay on psychographics and psychographic techniques; the procedure should be used to enrich the marketer's understanding of the people in the target markets. Although Rafiq and Ahmed (1993) might flinch, creation of a psychographic profile of a firm's employees (or the use of a commercially available scheme to create such a profile) seems to be a completely appropriate use of internal marketing.

Behavioral segmentation derives from the hypothesis that past behavior is a good indication of future behavior. Those who have bought Tide detergent in the past, for instance, are more likely to buy Tide detergent in the future than those who have not (always, of course, on the assumption that they have been pleased with the product). Therefore, it is relatively easy to create segments of probable users–one's past and current customers–and communication schemes to reach them. In fact, the whole foundation of database marketing or "integrated marketing"–the hot topic of the 1990s–is this hypothesis.

Part of the reason for this emphasis on past behavior is the fact that academic marketers have had a persistent problem: Attitudes research has been largely qualitative rather than quantitative and focused in strange directions. This has led to dissatisfaction with the field and the attempts to change attitudes. "Rather than change attitudes, [integrated marketing communications] seeks to change behavior. . . . We have never really been able to link attitudes to behavior" (Schultz, 1994). The only problem with this statement is that it is not true. Although it is true that psychologists and other behavioral scientists have had difficulties in so doing in laboratory settings, and marketers have tried to deal with "Attitude Toward the Ad" and whether a positive attitude leads toward purchase of the brand, those who work with people in a social service setting–ministers, social workers, doctors, etc.–know better. William Holliday, formerly the Senior Minister of Plymouth Church of Shaker Heights stated this fact bluntly in a sermon (1993): "Not only are attitudes cultivated by people; people are cultivated by attitudes, particularly when they have developed into habits." And habits, of course, are a specific form of behavior. This is a truth that parents readily understand.

So far I have been discussing only segmentation schemes that deal with individuals. Is it possible to segment groups of individuals, such as teams or companies? There have been tentative steps in this direction, made halting because of the underdeveloped nature of much of "industrial" marketing. The seminal article is Robertson and Wind (1980), wherein the authors attempt to create "organizational psychographics." Wasmer and Bruner (1991) go much further in attempting to segment employees within the service firm that share certain values and behaviors–even though they may not work together. This is done in an attempt to match rewards with behavior in a grid fashion (p. 41); they state that this operational scheme of organizational psychographics is most likely to succeed in multiple-site firms, but I fail to see why such is the case. It seems to me that multiple-department firms (such as banks and hospitals, to name only two industries that consist of organizations with large numbers of employees whose site is relatively compact) might have values shared within a department that were different enough from those of other departments to segment upon, as well as employees in different departments whose values were more similar with those in other departments than they were with employees in the same department. Nevertheless, I believe that Wasmer and Bruner's (1991) point about using organizational psychographics as a means of designing internal marketing strategies is important.

So where does all of this discussion of segmentation schemes leave us? This is not a course in Marketing 101, so I have not introduced the topic and varieties of segmentation methods merely to show off my years spent in the vineyards of the discipline. It is important for management to recognize the fact that not all of its employees are alike and that they will not all respond the same way to the same set of stimuli. If management truly desires to implement an internal marketing program, it is probably going to have to design a program that is flexible enough to provide different stimuli and benefits for different groups. And communicate those differences cogently so that the different target groups will each get the message intended for it–*and be able to ignore or not see and hear the messages intended for others, for those messages may be negative stimuli for a different target group*. This is not an easy assignment, but one which needs to be undertaken. And yet another reason, Rafiq and Ahmed (1993) notwithstanding, is that internal marketing needs to be a responsibility of marketing personnel and not human resources; human resources staff are not used to dealing with segmentation schemes–marketing people are.

Can a company successfully carry out an attempt to use segmentation schemes to mold opinion and communicate with employees nonmanipulatively? I would like to introduce a case, not one that was called an internal marketing program (the term was practically unknown at the time), but one that discusses an attempt to change organizational language and thought–which is part of most internal marketing efforts–and attempted to do so through the use of a segmentation scheme.

ORGANIZATIONAL CULTURE

Organizational culture is a problematic concept. There are probably as many definitions of organizational culture as there are academic authors who attempt to tackle the subject. Schein

(1985) defines it as a "pattern of basic assumptions" of a given group. Kilmann, Saxton, and Serpa (1986) define it as the "shared philosophies, ideologies, values, assumptions, beliefs, expectations, attitudes, and norms that knit a community together." Smircich (1983) reviews the concepts and definitions primarily in the organizational literature. Ouchi and Wilkins (1985) review the literature with an historical perspective, noting the shift of authors from faculty in sociology and anthropology departments to those disciplines that reside in management departments. And Deshpande and Webster (1989) attempt to move the definitions and concept of organizational culture over to marketing where its importance is "undeniable"; such work has been profitably continued by Slater and Narver (1993).

Culture per se is not all of what an individual knows and thinks and feels about his world–and thus organizational culture is not the sum of an individual's view of the organization(s) in which one finds oneself. "It is his *theory of what his fellows know, believe and mean,* his theory of the code being followed, the game being played, in the society into which he was born. . . ." (Kessing, 1981:58). Or, the organization in which one currently finds oneself.

Siehl and Martin (1990:269) state that

> if longitudinal data on culture and financial performance were available, important questions about causality could be addressed. For example, are informal behavioral norms generally stable over time independent of changes in formal policy? What is the lag between the adoption of a new cultural direction and its impact, if any, on financial performance? If there is an association between culture and financial performance, what is the direction of causality. . . .

The basic difficulty in defining organization culture seems to be that everyone "knows it when I see it," but there is little agreement on what it would consist of. Webster (1992) has made a step in the direction of enumerating the ingredients in a measurable fashion, creating a "Service Firm Marketing Culture Scale" and applying it in a case study. In what seems to be a backwards instance, Gummesson (1987) reports a case where internal marketing changed the culture in a firm. There is ample agreement, however, on culture's importance to the organization. And most people who have worked in more than one organization can discuss with some degree of intelligence the differences in various cultural dimensions among the organizations for which they have worked.

In their book, suggestively titled *The Tacit Organization* (1992), Ingersoll and Adams deal with the fact that organizations are symbolic enterprises as well as symbol-manipulating ones, and that we often cannot articulate that which we are closest to. I believe this accounts for much of the academics' problem with the concept of organizational culture. In fact, Ingersoll and Adams (1992) take the first 74 pages of their work, primarily a case study of how the Washington State Ferry System's culture evolved over a period of several generations, to discuss myth, "metamyth," and the role of children's literature (as exemplified by a series of stories published as Little Golden Books over the past 50 years) in creating an overall "managerial metamyth" into which most organizational cultures fit, at least in the United States.

Despite this academic difficulty in defining the term, managers seem intuitively to know exactly what "organizational culture" is and why it is important. Some of this knowledge undoubtedly is derived from *In Search of Excellence* (Peters and Waterman, 1982) and the ensuing books, articles, television programs, and news segments on "strong cultures" and their importance to American industry and competitiveness. (For a counter to some of this outpouring, see Saffold [1988].) What follows is a description of one company's organizational culture and the effects on that culture of a major change imposed by management.

DECOY AND VALS–A CASE STUDY

DECOY, Inc. was founded in the late 1950s to publish and print weekly newspapers. Always a technological leader, DECOY, Inc. was among the first printers outside the New York City area to use web-offset and cold type. In the 1960s, DECOY, Inc. entered the real estate publishing market with *Homes Illustrated,* magazines that depict houses for sale with both text and photographs and were distributed free to prospective homebuyers. By the late 1980s, DECOY, Inc. was publishing approximately 20 weekly suburban newspapers, 20 *Homes Illustrated* magazines, and one weekly real estate newspaper, covering cities from Southern California to northern Ohio.

DECOY, Inc. has continued in the technological forefront, and was among the first to use laser cameras and digital typesetting equipment. In 1977, DECOY, Inc. began the development of *CompuAd,* a computer program that writes classified advertisements for houses. By the late 1980s several hundred copies of *CompuAd* and its progeny had been sold in the United States and overseas.

The main reason for DECOY, Inc.'s success is, without a doubt, the Chairman and founder. The holder of degrees from two Ivy League colleges, he put together a successful company through a combination of hard work, vision, and top people who were both good at what they did and also complementary to the skills of the Chairman. By his own admission not much of an administrator, he also has an extremely low threshold of boredom. Therefore, his senior people need to have the ability to pick up his intellectual "dirty clothes" where he has dropped them and carry projects through to their conclusion. He has consistently been able to find such people.

The corporate culture of DECOY, Inc. in 1986 could only be described as open. The Chairman and other managers were readily accessible to everyone in the company. Further, there was little structure and no written job descriptions among senior managers. The concept of "corporate staff" did not exist, so almost anyone could be assigned to any special project–matrix management by default. The individual newspaper and magazine operations were highly autonomous, with next-to-no formal reporting requirements from the manager to the Chairman. Except for financial data, the only reporting consisted of telephone conversations, usually initiated by the Chairman when he wished to know "what's going on." Failure was rarely punished by termination; after 30 years in business, the Chairman was proud to announce that he had fired only two people. Displeasure was, rather, evidenced by a noticeable coolness in relations with the Chairman. People were intensely loyal to the Chairman; when a program of awarding service pins was initiated in 1989, several 25-year pins were given to relatively low-level employees.

A striking feature of the firm's culture was the fact that none of the entities identified itself as "A DECOY, Inc. Company" until many months or even years after the introduction of that name. All the entities were known by their own names and most of their local advertisers–and most of the advertisers for all the entities were local–thought the publications were locally owned. The DECOY, Inc. name was introduced, appeared on the mastheads of some of the publications, and no general explanation of what DECOY, Inc. was or why the name was being changed was ever made to either advertisers or employees. In early 1989, DECOY, Inc. started a newsletter to its almost-500 employees to present DECOY, Inc. and its entities to itself. It was with great reluctance that the Chairman was persuaded to write a couple of articles about who DECOY, Inc. was and why it mattered. He felt that these facts should be self-evident to his employees.

But the most noticeable feature of DECOY, Inc.'s culture was the firm's drive to innovate, both in improvements to current products and in the creation of new products. DECOY, Inc.'s innovation is directly attributable to the Chairman. Blessed with an inquiring mind, he continually asked questions beginning with "Why can't we?" or "Why doesn't?"–questions that often led to innovative solutions to problems. Because he let his managers manage, he had no difficulty "taking time from the same old grind" (Berton, 1989) for innovation. In fact, innovation frequently took precedence over operations, often to the distress of the managers.

DECOY, Inc. embodied several of Pearson's (1988) five key activities that make some firms innovators despite not having a clear structure or strategic focus. These activities are:

- Creating an environment that values performance above all else;
- Structuring to permit innovative ideas to rise above the demands of operations–or in this case, having no real structure;
- Defining a focus that lets the company channel its innovation realistically;
- Knowing where to look for good ideas;
- Going after good ideas full speed.

A danger of having the Chairman lead the innovation effort is that it becomes difficult to stop a bad idea, particularly when it is the Chairman's own. Staw (1976) and Staw and Ross (1987a, 1987b) have written extensively on escalation of commitment and its causes; DECOY, Inc. had continual difficulty in killing off projects that had become marginal, much less "bad" projects. This problem is possibly caused by the fact that the source of so much innovation at DECOY, Inc. is the Chairman.

DECOY, Inc. was in two quite different industries–newspapers and real estate publishing–and there was no common language across the industries. The only commonality was that both products were printed on newsprint. In one division the customers were almost exclusively real estate firms and their agents; in the other, customers were mostly retailers and individual subscribers. Both newspaper managers and *Homes Illustrated* managers had a good feel for what their advertisers wanted and needed, but used different terminology to articulate that feel to corporate staff. Communication as a cultural performance (Pacanowsky and O'Donnell-Trujillo, 1983) was difficult to decipher in these circumstances as there were multiple subcultures (if not true multiple cultures) within the firm. Thus, corporate staff wound up with a confused sense of who DECOY, Inc.'s customers were. This was not auspicious for continued long-term success (Miller, 1987) as the 1980s drew to a close.

SRI (formerly Stanford Research International) developed the Values and Life Styles Segmentation System (VALS) in the late 1970s. DECOY, Inc.'s Chairman first heard of VALS through an *Atlantic* magazine article (Atlas, 1984). His curiosity was aroused by VALS' purported ability to explain how "two people living next door to each other with the same basic demographic profile live so differently and buy such different things." Despite the presence of literally dozens of other typologies, VALS is well known by the business public and is relatively easy to explain to those who do not know it. These facts make it attractive to managers dealing with business-to-business marketing problems. After attending the VALS users' conference in November 1987, and finding himself in congenial company–an important consideration at DECOY, Inc.–the Chairman committed DECOY, Inc. to using VALS in the marketing of both *CompuAd* and *Homes Illustrated*.

The strategy for *CompuAd* was to use VALS to write more powerful and targeted advertisements. The computer would be programmed to create different advertisements for the same house to appeal to different VALS types. This ability would lead to more inquiries per ad, thus making *CompuAd* more valuable to its users. *Homes Illustrated* was to be redesigned to accommodate ads written for the different VALS types. DECOY, Inc. hoped that SRI's experience in real estate gained with their work with Ray Ellison Builders of San Antonio would help DECOY,

Inc. better focus its products and produce better advertising and promotional materials for the products.

DECOY, Inc.'s primary goal for using VALS was to have all its personnel speaking the same language about the firm's customers. James Tilton, then vice president at Ray Ellison Builders, claimed that the "greatest value of VALS is in sensitizing Ellison to the customers and *their* values" (Tilton, 1988)—not a goal to belittle in this day of better customer service and concern about "quality."

As part of the VALS subscription, DECOY, Inc. elected to have SRI come to Cleveland in February 1988, to deliver an orientation to most of the management of the corporation as well as the managers of the newspaper division. The VALS orientation included a slide show, videotapes, and role-playing exercises to familiarize individuals with the VALS types. At the end of the day-long session, most of the attendees had a rudimentary understanding of VALS and what the individuals of the various types were like.

DECOY, Inc. corporate staff was then charged with the task of developing an in-depth understanding of VALS to connect it to the various projects under way at DECOY, Inc. A great deal of hope was pinned upon VALS' being able to deliver a competitive edge to the electronic publishing ventures. By far the most important task was to disseminate the VALS language about customers and the population at large among DECOY, Inc.'s employees.

It was here that the first difficulty of the change effort occurred. It is easy to talk about "corporate" culture and "organizational" change; however, not every firm or agency is "organized." In fact, I steadfastly refused to refer to DECOY, Inc. as an "organization" and always categorized it as an Empire, with the model of the Holy Roman Empire in the late Middle Ages or the Van Sweringen corporate pyramid of the 1920s in mind (Haberman, 1979). I remember attending a meeting with DECOY, Inc.'s outside accountants and lawyers where we reviewed a spreadsheet purporting to show all of the entities in the Empire and the percentage of each that was owned by the Chairman. The accountants found an entity that had been omitted, as did the lawyers, as I did–but none of us knew about the entities the others found except the Chairman! Truly a Van Sweringenesque Empire.

DECOY, Inc. owned almost nothing; all of the entities were owned directly or indirectly by the chairman. The usual DECOY, Inc. practice for a new entity was to give the person with the idea (or a trusted local subordinate if the idea originated with DECOY, Inc.) potential ownership in a company of which the Chairman originally owned all, with the local person "sweating-in" earnings until he and the Chairman each owned 50 percent. DECOY, Inc. had been quite successful down through the years with this method. Although this may qualify as the "nation building" analogy that DiTomaso (1987) describes, it is so early in the process of nation building as to make it difficult to decide whether the resultant culture is "strong" or "weak."

All managers were given extreme latitude in running their operations: headquarters help was available if needed, but so long as the operation was profitable, supervision was minimal. Cross-communication, even within the same "division" was infrequent; managers usually communicated with headquarters which then disseminated information to the various operations. Attempting to impose change on this most loosely coupled of systems imaginable was not going to be easy.

And yet, there was immense change. DECOY, Inc.'s culture allowed for–in fact almost demanded–easy introduction of innovations. The Chairman's dictum that DECOY, Inc. would adopt VALS throughout the firm gave corporate staff the foot in the door with anyone who might be recalcitrant. Within a short time of the orientation meeting, all of DECOY, Inc.'s people were talking about "Belongers" and "Achievers" and "Soc Cons" ("Societally Conscious")–various segments in the VALS typology–as though these terms had been part of the DECOY,

Inc. lexicon forever. DECOY, Inc. *had* successfully adopted VALS as a corporate-wide language. Given a sufficient amount of time and effort, it should have been possible to make the sophisticated use of the typology second nature to key employees at most of the entities. The managers had, without realizing it, been crying out for such a communications tool for a long time. These managers were a willing body of disciples for adoption.

However, to the disappointment of both corporate staff and the Chairman, the ancillary uses of VALS came to naught at DECOY, Inc. There were only two rather feeble attempts to VALS-type markets for DECOY, Inc. products. A haphazardly chosen sample of *CompuAd* users was VALS typed with marginal results and no follow-through. Readers of one DECOY, Inc. newspaper who requested information were sent a VALS-typing questionnaire to be returned. There was no follow-through with these returned questionnaires. Markets were to be VALS-typed prior to the introduction of two new products as a now-standard part of the new product research and development process. When the new product introductions were stopped, so was the VALS typing. An abortive attempt to do a "quick-and-dirty" VALS typing at an interactive computer terminal for a new product was stopped before the algorithms were sketched.

Several attempts were made to tie VALS directly into one of the newspapers and the *CompuAd* family of products—primarily through the use of words, symbols, or design elements which would appeal to one or more of the types. A prototype of a future NewsAd could write two advertisements for the same house for different VALS types—one for Achievers and one for the Societally Conscious—with a single input of data, thus proving that the concept was sound. An advertisement for NewsAd 2 was directed squarely at Achievers. And, when a major new marketing effort was launched in 1989 for NewsAd 2, a pair of media advertisements was produced, one aimed at Achievers and the other at the Societally Conscious. These were the most promising developments of VALS "technology" in regard to the DECOY, Inc. product line.

However, two events intervened in 1989 to bring these developments to a halt. First, in January 1989, SRI introduced VALS 2, a whole new typology that bore little resemblance to VALS. It remains to be seen what impact the new typology will have on the marketing and consumer behavior fields. Because it is based on "unchanging psychological stances rather than shifting values and lifestyles" (Riche, 1989:30), VALS 2 should enhance the ability of subscribers to predict behavior–always a problem with VALS.

DECOY, Inc. was not enchanted with the change. Some of the corporate staff were quite bitter that the change was introduced just at the point that DECOY, Inc. was about to truly utilize VALS. To echo the words of Chevron Corporation's Manager of Research, DECOY, Inc. was not sure that VALS was so broken as to need fixing–at least not with VALS 2 (Winters, 1989).

Second, in November 1989, for a number of compelling corporate reasons, DECOY, Inc. stopped marketing the NewsAd family of products, the last of the products that VALS was supposed to help. As a result of these factors, DECOY, Inc. elected not to renew its subscription to VALS 2.

Was DECOY, Inc.'s VALS attempt worth the effort? The unifying factor of a common language provided a large enough benefit by itself to make the effort not only worthwhile, but a success. DECOY, Inc. did not make any more marketing use of its adoption of VALS than it did of its own name change. Most DECOY, Inc. customers did not know that the firm was a VALS subscriber, nor were they advised how to use VALS in *their* marketing efforts. VALS was never adequately used to gain a competitive edge for DECOY, Inc. One reason for this fact was the introduction of VALS 2 so soon after DECOY, Inc. subscribed to VALS. A second reason was the culture at DECOY, Inc. where operational decisions were left to the entities and not dictated by headquarters. When the entities raised potential uses for VALS, the Chairman never stated that he espoused such use. Despite all the shortcomings in the implementation of VALS, in SRI's handling of its product, and in VALS itself, the effort at least operated at "break-even" and probably was a net benefit in allowing this highly fragmented firm to communicate better internally, even if the external communications possibilities of the introduction of VALS and selling the concept of using VALS in the customers' advertisements with their customers never developed.

Some of the most pressing questions in any discussion in administration or "action research" are "Will this intervention work?" "Can a variable be manipulated?" "Can a firm change its culture?" These questions may be too large to ever be answered–and certainly beyond my capability to answer–and from the present instance the answer would seem to be "no." DECOY, Inc. remains today a highly fragmented, open firm, treasuring innovation, and as unable to communicate internally as ever. New production methods are being introduced and new products and services are being developed and used. In many ways, DECOY, Inc. seems to be just as it was prior to the attempted introduction of VALS.

Certain elements of a company's culture can be changed, however. DECOY, Inc.'s entity managers showed no hesitation in adopting "VALS-speak" when it was championed by the Chairman. VALS as both a language and as a description of the world was accepted, not only because "the Chairman said so," but also for other reasons. First, as mentioned above, it filled a need which many of the managers had already felt. Second, and possibly just as important, it was seen as a way for DECOY, Inc. to join the "big boys" who were VALS users. As such, it fit within a cultural norm of the firm–to be innovative, to matter. As an aside, DECOY, Inc., has recently contracted with Gallup Research, Inc., to perform some readership research on some of its publications. Again, although the research methodology promises to produce interesting results which DECOY, Inc., can use profitably if it can implement the results properly, it is the attraction of the Gallup name that was the final selling point for the research. "Everyone knows Gallup," the Chairman has said repeatedly; this is another example of DECOY's joining the "big boys," regardless of the research results.

As a final word on the subject, I would like to address a potential concern involved in any attempt to change culture. Many academic writers have properly questioned the ethics of attempted cultural change by managerial "elites." In the DECOY, Inc. case, some of the ethical considerations are obviated by the fact that the Chairman owned 100 percent of the stock in DECOY, Inc. and had the acquiescence in adopting VALS by the remaining owners of the other firms in the "Empire." In a sense, DECOY, Inc. is thus different from the usual firm written about in the management literature–particularly the literature of organizational culture and culture change–in *not* being a large, widely owned firm whose managers are not the owners of a significant share of the stock. In the case of DECOY, Inc., the Chairman had the legal right to adopt VALS in an attempt to change the organizational culture if he wanted; if the rest of the employees did not like the choice, they could leave. This legal argument, of course, does not answer the questions of right versus ethical process. As Wilkins and Dyer (1988) state, various cultures change in various ways; the type of legal/cultural matrix discussed here changed in some of its parts without a great deal of resistance to that change.

Can culture be manipulated? The DECOY, Inc., case shows that where ownership is concentrated in the hands of management, where employees are loyal to management, and where management does not try to turn the total culture in a diametrically opposed direction to its current posture in a short time, cultural *elements* can be purposefully manipulated. This of course does not answer the ethical question posed above about whether the culture *should* be manipulated or not–it simply says that parts of the culture *can be* deliberately changed. If the culture can be purposefully changed by management, can it also be inadvertently changed? Probably. Can it be changed, either purposefully or inadvertently, by actions from below, by the employees? I would have to say without a doubt that such actions are not only possible, but occur frequently.

Chapter 4

How Do We Market?

ORGANIZING TO MARKET: THREE METHODS OF ORGANIZATION DESIGN

When one discusses practical services marketing, as opposed to what the theoretical considerations might be and regardless of how manufacturing and other kinds of firms are organized (Schneider, 1987), three models for designing the marketing effort spring to mind. First is the Account Manager, familiar from advertising agencies and similar organizations. Second is the Relationship Manager, familiar from recent developments in banking, but equally familiar to those who know social workers–or trust officers who are actually overpaid, underworked social workers. Third is what I call "Interlocking Spiderwebs," where the person or persons responsible for marketing serve to tie various relationships together.

The Account Manager operates as the client's contact into a specific part of the organization. This was how the trust departments at both banks where I worked were organized; I was responsible for a list of accounts–up to almost 200–and was supposed to know enough about only their employee benefit trust business to take care of their employee benefit trust business and perhaps develop a bit more employee benefit trust business from them. But not personal trust business from their employees or general banking business from either the firm or its employees; those sales responsibilities lay elsewhere at the bank. And any marketing materials were to be developed by the bank's marketing department–which at best could be described as not understanding the trust business in general and the employee benefit trust business was totally incomprehensible to them.

This method of organizing a marketing effort has always struck me as less than optimal. It has also struck others that way, so the concept of relationship management arose to solve this particular organizational design problem. The Relationship Manager operates as a customer's point-of-entry into an entire organization, regardless of what service that client needs. Customers are instinctively drawn to the relationship manager concept; they resent having to deal with many people from a service provider, each with his or her own little slice of expertise and vision about the customer's organization. The Relationship Manager becomes the lead person, knowing more about the customer and his or her business than anyone else in the organization; truly the Relationship Manager is operating in the realm beyond individual competence and in the area of maximizing total organizational revenue.

If properly handled, it does not matter where in the provider organization the Relationship Manager is housed; the manager should probably be affiliated with the department that provides the most service to a particular customer, so that the department the Relationship Manager works in would vary from one customer to the next. The important thing is that the customer only calls the Relationship Manager, not individual departments in the provider organization (unless the question or problem is a minor, operational one); otherwise, the Relationship Manager would lose control over the relationship. The true focus of the Relationship Manager thus becomes one of communication manager. Communications need to be relevant and two-way, allowing the organization to speak with one voice to a customer.

Relationship Management should not be confused with the currently fashionable concept of "Relationship Marketing." The best definition of relationship marketing that I have seen is that it is (Shani and Chalasani, 1992:34):

> an integrated effort to identify, maintain, and build up a network with individual consumers and to continuously strengthen the network for the mutual benefit of both sides, through interactive, individualized and value-added contacts over a long period of time.

This definition seems to require a different, newer, method of organization, discussed below.

In an article which attacks marketing's sacred "4 Ps," Gronroos (1994) claims that relationship marketing is the emerging paradigm for marketing. It is becoming the foundation for a theory of marketing that he maintains is lacking. He claims that relationship marketing will develop into a new way of managing marketing problems; by changing the focus of the firm from transaction driven to relationship driven, the new paradigm will increase firm's long-term profitability. One underpinning of relationship marketing is an internal marketing program. Figure 4.1 outlines the strategic differences between transaction-oriented marketing and relationship-oriented marketing.

However, despite Gronroos's cogent delineation of relationship marketing, it is not without its detractors and its pitfalls. Rosenfield (1994) lists nine "hidden dangers" that can befall any relationship-marketing effort:

1. Assuming that customers want a relationship.
2. Assuming that customers are willing to work.
3. Assuming that customers will be fair.
4. Assuming that customer satisfaction is enough.
5. There will be a tendency to tier upward.
6. There will be accidental disenfranchisement.
7. Rules may change, causing dissatisfaction.
8. There may be cannibalization of existing business, with no incremental gain.
9. The program may mistake necessity for loyalty.

FIGURE 4.1. Gronroos' Marketing-Strategy Continuum

The strategy continuum	Transaction marketing	Relationship marketing
Time perspective	Short-term focus	Long-term focus
Dominating marketing function	Marketing mix	Interactive marketing (supported by marketing mix activities)
Price elasticity	Customers tend to be more sensitive to price	Customers tend to be less sensitive to price
Dominating quality dimension	Quality of output (technical quality dimension) is dominating	Quality of interactions (functional quality dimension) grows in importance and may become dominating
Measurement of satisfaction	Monitoring market share (direct approach)	Managing the customer base (direct approach)
Customer information system	*Ad hoc* customer satisfaction surveys	Real-time customer feedback system
Interdependency between marketing, operations, and personnel	Interface of no or limited strategic importance	Interface of substantial strategic importance
The role of internal marketing	Internal marketing of no or limited importance to success	Internal marketing of substantial strategic importance to success

The product continuum	Computer packaged goods	→←	Consumer durables	→←	Industrial goods	→←	Services

Source: Gronroos, Chris, (1994). "From Marketing Mix to Relationship Marketing: Towards a Paradigm Shift in Marketing," *Management Decision*, Vol. 32, #2.

Some of these hidden dangers apply more to "loyalty programs" such as the airlines' frequent flyer programs than relationship marketing *per se*. Nevertheless, they are potential problems for service marketers. The assumption that customers will be fair underlies the unconditional service guarantee program discussed below. The assumption that people will be willing to work underlies the trend to getting customers to perform some of the service. I believe that Gronroos is correct in his emphasis on relationship marketing; however, Rosenfield's points are well taken and need to be remembered by any firm seeking to establish a relationship marketing program.

Given the fact that customers are intuitively drawn to the relationship management form of organization, the advantages to the organization of using Relationship Managers rather than Account Managers in each department cannot be overemphasized. A case example from my personal history will illustrate this fact. I left Central National Bank's trust department, as mentioned previously, and went to Society National Bank to work in the same capacity–in a bank totally organized hierarchically around Account Managers. After I had been at Society for a couple of months, the owner of one of the firms whose profit-sharing plan I administered called and said that because I was paying a lot of attention to him–more than ever before (I should have–I had almost nothing else to do)–he wanted to send more of his business over to Society from Cleveland Trust where it was currently located. He had just bought a house and needed a $200,000+ mortgage; who should he talk to? I told him that I didn't know, but that I would quickly find out and have that person give him a call.

I found out, talked to the person in mortgage banking, gave him a few details, such as "Don't turn this person down without talking to me because he has a large employee benefit trust on my desk," and told him to call the customer. Two weeks later, my customer called and asked when the person from mortgage banking was going to call him. I said that I would get right on it and make sure that he called while I was standing beside his desk. My customer told me not to bother, as Cleveland Trust had given him a new mortgage, no questions asked, but insisted that he give them more of his banking business. Because Society's mortgage banking department had failed, the trust department lost an account which paid over $1,000 per year in fee income. Had Society been organized around the relationship manager concept, it is unlikely that this account would have departed.

Relationship management should deal with developing targeted offers to particular customers or segments to derive incremental sales from them. Further, it can launch preferred-customer programs for your best customers and remind customers that there is an opportunity cost for failure to stay loyal—and provide ongoing incentives for that loyalty.

Much of the former resistance to relationship management was predicated upon difficulties of communication and in knowing what was going on with a customer who might do business with half-dozen departments (or more) in a large organization. New technologies, mostly related to personal computers, have changed things, thereby allowing a Relationship Manager to know what is going on in a fairly large list of accounts, and facilitating extensive and complicated business with any organization. This, of course, does not mean that Relationship Managers *will* know what is going on; simply that they *can* be given the tools to know. It is now possible and fairly easy to organize a firm so that it is truly customer driven, not service driven (Peppers and Rogers, 1993). If, to continue the bank story a bit further, a trust customer of mine wants to provide MasterCard for his employees, I, as Relationship Manager, should be able to expedite the transaction, rather than have a representative from MasterCard treat the account as a new entity. Customers hate that. I had customers at both banks who routinely complained about the seven, eight, and in one case, ten departments of the bank that they had to deal with, each with turnover problems and different reporting cycles and requirements. Customers in the 1990s are beyond being willing to tolerate this type of operation; they insist on relationship management.

But relationship management describes only what is going on currently as, almost, "best practice." Where are we headed with customer management? I believe that the future will bring about a new method of organizing that I call "Interlocking Spiderwebs."

"Interlocking Spiderwebs" occur at those points where organizations interact with each other to provide services to customers. My firm, North Union Associates, has the capability to provide extensive computer consulting, deliver personal computers to an organization, perform network maintenance, write programs, etc., even though none of my employees can do any of these things. How? Simply because I have a colleague with whom I have worked in the past who does all of the above tasks for his firm and who would subcontract for North Union at the drop of a hat. My client would probably not care that Bob was not an employee of my firm and might not even know his status. Similarly, I can deliver industrial design capabilities, accounting and auditing work, and several other specialties to clients through North Union, simply because I sit in the middle of a web of relationships with other service providers who would work through my firm. My clients have, on occasion, made use of this method of working with people who I recommended. I believe that this method of delivering services, especially professional services, will continue to grow in the years ahead.

This new method of organizing plays upon several trends that have been important in the past. It allows firms to reduce their own payroll and still maintain pools of talent that they can call upon on a needs-only basis. It also is happening now because of the successful application and integration of technology that has been developed in the past decade. All too many technological investments have simply automated what the firm was doing; we are finally beginning to see the introduction of technologies that allow firms to redesign what they do and how they do it. Much technology investment has been made to automate transactions and transaction processing; this is particularly true in many service industries and is probably one of the reasons that service productivity gains have not been better over the years. We are finally starting to see investments in new technology which will allow firms to manage relationships more effectively (Axson, 1992).

Interlocking Spiderwebs deliver the best of the trust officer of old. He or she was expected to do what the customer wanted and what was best for the customer, no matter whether it was in the best interests of the institution for which he or she ultimately worked. Theoretically, trust officers were expected to get the best checking account for their customers, for instance, regardless of which bank offered the best account. Despite this theory, it has always been extremely rare for a bank trust officer to open a checking account in another bank, for cash balances are the lifeblood of banks (*Abuse on Wall Street,* 1980). And customers recognized that they were possibly not getting quite as good a deal on each individual service as they might if they were willing to shop for it themselves; however, one of the reasons for having a trust in a trust department has always been to reduce the need to do things oneself, to have one contact person for all of the services trust department representatives provide. But the person who organizes along these lines does not have the built-in institutional conflicts of interest that a bank trust department has. For instance, although I have a preferred industrial design firm to use, if a client wants to use another (primarily because my preferred firm is somewhat expensive in the short run), I do not mind, as I do not receive any revenue from whichever firm is used. Although *my* life is made easier by using my preferred firm, I have successfully worked with other firms.

And this is what the Interlocking Spiderweb method of organizing service delivery can do. As with a very large firm one person can deliver a wide range of services to clients even though that person may actually perform only a very small slice of the total services provided for that customer. The range of services so provided is limited only those individuals the person knows well enough to guarantee their work–for their work will be done in the name of that person (or his or her firm) and that person's guarantee will extend to that work; however, despite the potential problems, this method of organizing has a great deal to offer service providers.

COMMUNICATION STRATEGIES

The most important question to answer after "How do we market?" is "How do we communicate with our market?" Having discussed segmentation strategies and methods in Chapter 3, we now need to discuss how to communicate with the segments we have created. It makes little or no sense to segment a market–either internal or external–by demographics, geographics, psychographics, or tea leaves, and then communicate with the segments as if all the segments were alike. Therefore, a good communications strategy needs to segment the communications in a way that the appropriate message for each segment is communicated to that segment appropriately, with as little "spillover" to another segment as possible.

Fortunately, such a technique is readily available in the Myers-Briggs Type Indicator (MBTI). Strongly grounded, not in Freudian psychology, but in the work of Carl Jung, the MBTI has been around for decades (Myers and McCaulley, 1985). It is quite possible that you have not heard of it both because it is only now gaining academic respectability due to its lack of Freudian base) and the fact that its strongest supporters have for years been educators.

The MBTI, a fairly long (126-item) psychological testing instrument, separates people into "Types" along four dimensions: Perception (Sensing or Intuition); Judgment (Thinking or

Feeling); Attitude (Extroversion or Introversion); and Orientation to the Outer World (Judgment or Perception). There is not a hint in either Jungian theory or in the MBTI itself that one type is "better" than another; no "therapist" will try to "cure" you of your type. This is one of the appeals of type theory as opposed to Freudian psychology: it deals with healthy people. After responding to the instrument, people are then classified into one of 16 types based upon which of the items in each dimension is dominant (see Figure 4.2). For instance, my Type is INTJ: I am an Introvert (as defined by Jung–I also am introverted according to the normal definition, but the two do not necessarily go together); I perceive things Intuitively (with my brain and not with my hands–I am not an experimenter); my judgments are based on internal Thinking, not concern with how others feel (as many people will certainly testify); and my orientation to the outer world is Judgment-based.

Great! Now what? There has been quite a lot written on MBTI, describing the 16 Types, how Type connects with Temperament, what does it all mean, etc. There is a national Association–the Association for Psychological Type–that publishes extensively and sponsors a biennial scholarly conference complete with papers on many subjects connected with type theory and practice. There are dozens of books on the subject in general; probably the best source for the older material is Myers (1980). One can get into this as deeply as one wants; however, my goal here is to deal with the use of the MBTI in organizations and as a tool for improving an organization's communications. There is a significant amount of material here, too. In fact, there is even an MBTI instrument for typing Teams and Groups as a whole, although I have no experience with it, nor have I read any reports based upon its use.

Table 4.1 outlines the preferred methods of communication along each of the dimensions (interestingly, *not* by the 16 types). It is fairly clear that communicating to the people in an organiza-

FIGURE 4.2. The Sixteen Types

		SENSING TYPES		INTUITIVE TYPES			
		WITH THINKING	WITH FEELING	WITH FEELING	WITH THINKING		
INTROVERTS	JUDGING	**ISTJ**	**ISFJ**	**INFJ**	**INTJ**	JUDGING	INTROVERTS
INTROVERTS	PERCEPTIVE	**ISTP**	**ISFP**	**INFP**	**INTP**	PERCEPTIVE	INTROVERTS
EXTROVERTS	PERCEPTIVE	**ESTP**	**ESFP**	**ENFP**	**ENTP**	PERCEPTIVE	EXTROVERTS
EXTROVERTS	JUDGING	**ESTJ**	**ESFJ**	**ENFJ**	**ENTJ**	JUDGING	EXTROVERTS

TABLE 4.1. Preferred Methods of Communications

Extroversion	Introversion
Communicate energy and enthusiasm	Keep energy and enthusiasm inside
Respond quickly	Like to think before responding
Focus of talk is on people and things	Focus is on internal ideas and thoughts
Need to moderate expression	Need to be drawn out
Seek to communicate in groups	Seek to communicate one to one
Prefer face-to-face to written	Prefer written to face-to-face
Sensing	Intuition
Like evidence presented first	Like global schemes presented first
Want practical applications	Want possible future challenges discussed
Rely on direct experience	Rely on insights and imagination
Use orderly step-by-step approach in presentations	Use round-about approach in presentations
Follow agenda in meetings	Bypass agenda in meetings
Refer to specific examples	Refer to general concepts
Thinking	Feeling
Prefer to be brief and concise	Prefer to be sociable and friendly
Want the pros and cons listed	Want to know how alternatives effect people
Convinced by cool impersonal reasoning	Convinced by personal information
Present goals and objectives first	Present points of agreement first
Consider emotions and feelings as data to weigh	Consider logic and objectivity as data to value
Seek involvement with tasks in meetings	Seek involvement with people in meetings
Judgment	Perception
Want to discuss schedules and timetables	Want to discuss schedules but are uncomfortable with deadlines
Dislike surprises	Enjoy surprises
Expect others to follow through	Expect others to adapt to situational requirements
State positions and decisions clearly	Present their views as tentative and modifiable
Communicate results and achievements	Communicate options and opportunities
Talk of purpose and direction	Talk of autonomy and flexibility
Focus on task to be done	Focus on process to be appreciated

Source: Pridgen (1988:30)

tion is not as simple as posting a notice on the bulletin board, at least if you want everyone to understand what it is you mean. Given the fact that most organizations of any size at all will employ people from many of the types, it becomes apparent that a communication strategy must be developed that approaches talking with each group quite differently. Yeakley (1982) warns against accepting too quickly the hypothesis that type similarity equals easier and better communications.

This is true even if the people you want to talk to fall into the same group along other dimensions or in other segmentation schemes. Several years ago, DECOY, Inc., retained National Market Measures, a Cleveland market-research firm, to do focus groups for three VALS groups on how they reacted to different house styles. A focus group was convened for Achievers, Belongers, and the two Inner-Directed groups. The latter two groups were successful and provided a great deal of information. The Achiever group was a total flop; according to the moderator, it was the most difficult group to run that she had ever encountered, because they simply would not follow up with each other and tended to answer in two- or three-word sentences. We sent the tape of this group to SRI for their comments; the analyst called me immediately with his comment, chuckling. "You ran into a bad MBTI pattern. Run the group again." We did, with much more success. Same psychographic profile, different communication pattern.

Yeakley (1983:22-23) presents four listening styles that have tremendous importance for designing communications strategies. Listening in the sensing style means interpreting at a practical level and asking such questions as: What is the speaker saying? How should the words be decoded? How should the message be perceived? Listening in the intuitive style means understanding at a much deeper level than the sensing style and asking such questions as: What does the speaker really mean? What are the assumptions underlying the message? What are the message's implications? What are the possibilities suggested by the message? Listening in the thinking style means analyzing and organizing while asking such questions as: What is the message's structure? What is its central idea? What are its main points and subpoints and how are they related? Is there adequate evidence to justify each claim? Is the reasoning logical? Are the claims true or false? Listening in the feeling style means evaluating and appreciating while asking such questions as: What values are suggested by the message? Should these values be accepted or rejected? How do I feel about the message? How do I feel about the speaker? The true significance of Yeakley's article is that most of us use different listening styles at different times; we may *tend* to listen in the thinking style, but we *can* and *do* listen in other styles. It is therefore incumbent upon those designing communications strategies and executions to be aware of this fact and deal with it, making it possible for us either to stay in our preferred style or go to another listening style if it is evidently appropriate for the particular message.

McBride and Cline (1989) report on a campaign designed by students at Southwest Texas State University for Apple Computer (at Apple's request); the campus campaign was to increase awareness of Apple Macintosh's benefits, increase knowledge of the Apple Purchase Program, and announce Apple's new student financing program. The students utilized several type-discovering techniques to infer the dominant types on campus and designed their campaign to match those types. The campaign was very successful, and the authors attribute this mostly to the fact that the students were able to match the communications approach of the advertising campaign with the psychological types on campus.

How to discover your employees' Types? Giving the MBTI to all employees is the obvious choice; it is not difficult nor expensive to administer–less than $5.00 per employee plus the fee for the psychologist to administer it if no one in your firm is so licensed (Consulting Psychologists Press is the source for the instrument). However, some employees would possibly object to the test and being typed–even though the MBTI, not being a therapy-based instrument, treats all the types as equally valid and no one type is "better" than any other. It is possible to infer people's types from their overt behavior; this technique was developed by educators whose students were too young to take the test (Lawrence, 1982). Although not all of the checklists in Table 4.2 have been field tested, they do seem to work; if one is familiar with type theory and practice, of course, they would work better. One should also remember that these items were designed for teachers to use; although managers should be at least as able to "read" their employees (and bosses) as teachers are able to "read" their students, they do tend to be looking for different traits.

After reading Tables 4.1 and 4.2 the question inevitably arises as to the possibility of getting to a person's MBTI "backwards"–that is, are people in a group more likely to have the same type. To a certain extent the answer seems to be yes. McDaid, McCaulley, and Kainz (1986) represent an attempt to digest the results of the thousands of people who have taken the MBTI down through the years. The total Center for Psychological Type data bank population of MBTI records consists of 232,557 records for the years 1971 to 1984; the distribution of types ranges from a low of ESTP (3.08 percent) to a high of ENFP (10.52 percent) of the population. There were 59,784 records with usable occupational codes and the Atlas (1984) attempts to deal with these. For instance, accountants (N = 427) are ESTJ (20.14 percent–next highest category is ENTJ with 12.41 percent); almost half of CPAs (N = 494) fall into these two categories–26.72 percent and 19.23 percent respectively; marketing personnel (N = 83) are ENTJ (15.66 percent) and ENTP (13.25 percent), with reasonably similar concentrations of ESTP, ENFP, and ESTJ all over 9 percent; salesworkers (N = 1750) were ESTJ (12.69 percent),

TABLE 4.2. Observation of Type Inferences

If your employee is an EXTROVERT, it is likely that he or she
Chooses to work with a group
Plunges into new experiences
Is relaxed and self-confident
Is interested in others and their doings
Readily offers opinions
Shares personal experiences
Wants to experience things so as to understand them
Asks questions to check on the expectations of the group or leader
Has a relatively short attention span
Dislikes complicated procedures and gets impatient with slow jobs
Eagerly attends to interruptions
Acts quickly, often without thinking
Likes to work by trial and error

If your employee is an INTROVERT, it is likely that he or she
Likes to work alone
Holds back from new experiences
Chooses written assignments
Pauses before answering and shows discomfort with spontaneous questioning
Asks questions to understand something before attempting to do it
Seems "deep"
Is intense
Prefers setting own standards when possible
Likes quiet space in which to work
Works intently on the task at hand
Works on one thing at a time
Dislikes interruptions
May spend too much time in thought and neglect to get started

If your employee prefers SENSING, it is likely that he or she
Is realistic and practical
Is more observant than imaginative
Enjoys owning things and making them work
Prefers memorizing to finding reasons
Learns best from an orderly sequence of details
Interested in facts
Keeps accurate track of details, is a listmaker
Is patient
Is good at precise work
Likes to know the "right way" to solve problems
Likes an established routine
Works steadily, not in fits and starts
Is impatient or frustrated with complicated situations

If your employee prefers INTUITION, it is likely that he or she

Seems to like something new all the time
Is more imaginative than observant
Attends more to the concept than the details
Becomes restless and impatient with routine
Is an initiator, innovator
Sees possibilities that others miss
Is quick with finding solutions
Doesn't always hear you out; anticipates your words
Likes problems that require new ways of being solved
Dislikes precise work with many details
Enjoys learning a new skill more than using it
Works in bursts of energy with slack periods between
Jumps to conclusions, makes factual errors
Finds reading easy

If your employee prefers THINKING, it is likely that he or she

Wants logical reasons before accepting new ideas
Tries to be fair
Is impersonal and objective
Finds ideas and things more interesting than people
Is more truthful than tactful
Is brief and businesslike
Takes facts, theories, and the discovery of truth very seriously
Treats emotional relationships and ideals casually
Contributes intellectual criticism
Exposes wrongs in the habits and beliefs of others
Is offended by illogic
Holds firmly to a policy or conviction
Hurts other people's feelings without knowing it
Has a low need for harmony
Is upset by injustice

If your employee prefers FEELING, it is likely that he or she

Is personable
Is more interested in people than things
Is more tactful than truthful
Is likely to agree with others in the group
Thinks as others think, believing them to be probably right
Finds it difficult to be brief and businesslike
Takes emotional relationships and ideals very seriously
Is offended by a lack of personal consideration in others
Is motivated by others
May comply or conform to avoid disharmony
Permits feelings to override logic

TABLE 4.2 (continued)

Forecasts how others will feel
Arouses enthusiasm
Is upset by conflict, values harmony
Dislikes telling people unpleasant things
Is sympathetic

If your employee is a JUDGING type, it is likely that he or she
Likes to have things decided and settled
Is more decisive than curious
Lives according to plans
Lives according to standards and customs not easily or lightly set aside
Tries to makes situations conform to own standards
Makes definite choices from among the possibilities
Is uneasy with unplanned happenings
Bases friendships upon shared beliefs, standards, and tastes
Has enduring friendships
Sets up "shoulds" and "oughts" and judges self against them
Aims to be right
Is self-regimented, purposeful, and exacting
Is orderly, organized, and systematic
Likes assignments to be clear and definite
Has settled opinions
May be tolerant of routine procedure

If your employee is a PERCEPTIVE type, it is likely that he or she
Is more curious than decisive
Lives according to the situation of the moment
May not plan things but act spontaneously
Is comfortable in handling the unplanned
Looks for new experiences and expects to be interested
Samples many more experiences than can be digested or used
Takes a "live and let live" attitude
Bases friendships on propinquity and shared experiences
Takes on friendships easily
Aims to miss nothing
Is flexible, adaptable, and tolerant
Wants to understand things more than manage them
Leaves things open
Has trouble making decisions
Starts too many projects and has difficulty finishing them
Postpones unpleasant jobs
Welcomes new light on a thing or situation

Source: Lawrence (1982:69-77)

ENFP (11.03 percent), and ESFJ (10.06 percent). Further, Brock and Demarest (1989) report a method for using type theory and observation of client's behavior to infer their type in an effort to sell better to each type; Twining (1990) presents another approach to sales training. For further details see Myers and Myers, 1980.

In fact, SRI did some work about VALS Types and MBTI Types in an attempt to link the two (Warrick, 1984). Key findings of that research were that the outer directed VALS Types (Belongers and Achievers in particular) were more Extroversion-oriented, whereas the inner-directed VALS Types (Societally Conscious and Experiential in particular) were more Introversion oriented. Eighty-two percent of the outer directed were Sensing; 52 percent of the inner directed were Intuitive. Thus it is possible to *infer* whether an individual is inner directed or outer directed by observation along the dimensions of Table 4.2.

So what? Where are we going? Simply stated, in order to put a potentially successful internal marketing program into placc, onc needs to segment one's employees into meaningful groups (similar to VALS if not that exact scheme) and determine what communications strategies to use to reach each of those groups, because if the groups are divided meaningfully, the method of communication successfully used with one group will fail abysmally when used for another.

TRAINING STRATEGIES

This is where the emphasis shifts from managers as administrators and supervisors to managers as teachers. I mentioned earlier that the mainstays of MBTI applications have been educators. Teachers of students at every level will state unequivocally that people learn differently; this is an experience-based statement. Parents of multiple children may have noticed this fact, unless their children all have learned alike. Use of the MBTI has allowed teachers, particularly elementary and middle-school teachers, to codify these differences and learn how to teach to children in each of the different types. Remember, *each type is equally valid.* As a sometime college teacher I have difficulty with this fact, because frequently what I am teaching–particularly finance–cannot readily be learned in multiple ways and because of my psychological type, I have difficulty in seeing alternative methods of instruction. Further, nothing in the concept of psychological type implies that the content of a lesson or communication needs to be "dummied down" for any psychological type; it simply says that different types learn the same lesson content differently.

Let me give a series of three examples of how a teacher can transform a basic lesson so that any of the students can understand, learn from it, and deal with the identical content. Although through good training and study, one can be aware of all 16 types and their identifying characteristics, it is difficult for even the best of us to plan a good communications strategy to enable us to reach them all; further, it is possibly not even necessary to do so, for it is possible that the discrimination necessary to separate the 16 types from each other on the typing instrument is impossible in real life. Therefore, methods to cluster the types into a smaller number of similar groups have been developed (*The Type Reporter*, 1985): The Four Quadrants, the Four Temperaments, and the Four Columns (see Figure 4.3). Each of these techniques takes two of the attributes that are alike–and generally two that are more important than the others–and addresses communications to those attributes.

The Four Quadrants approach starts with the fact that people in each quadrant learn better through techniques that are different from those of the other quadrants: Extroverts with Sensing learn best through hands-on activities that involve more than one person; Introverts with Sensing learn best through hands-on activities that can be done alone or with one person; Extroverts with

FIGURE 4.3. Three Ways to Look at Your Students

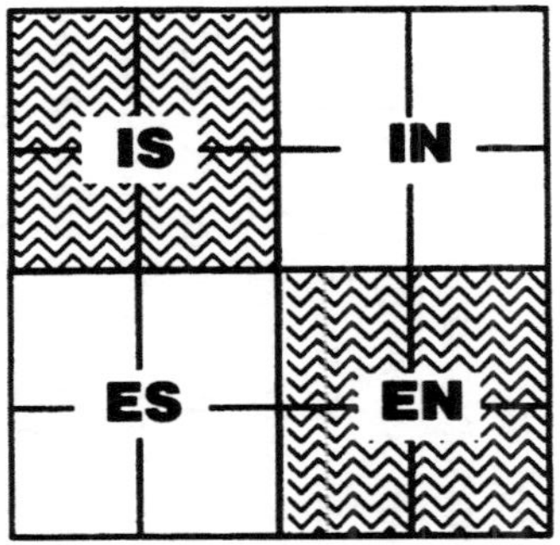

1. Through the Four Quadrants

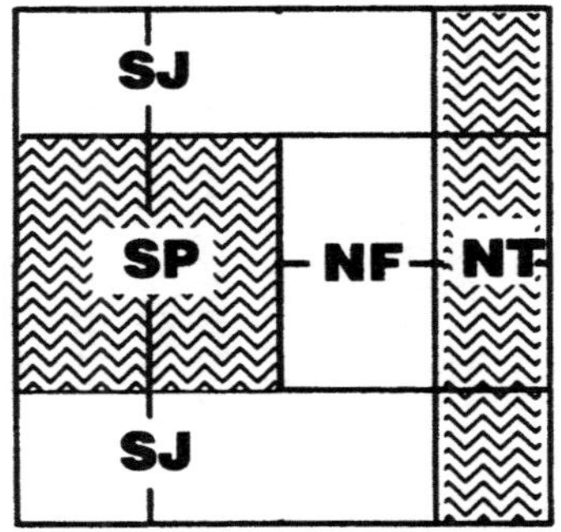

2. Through the Four Temperaments

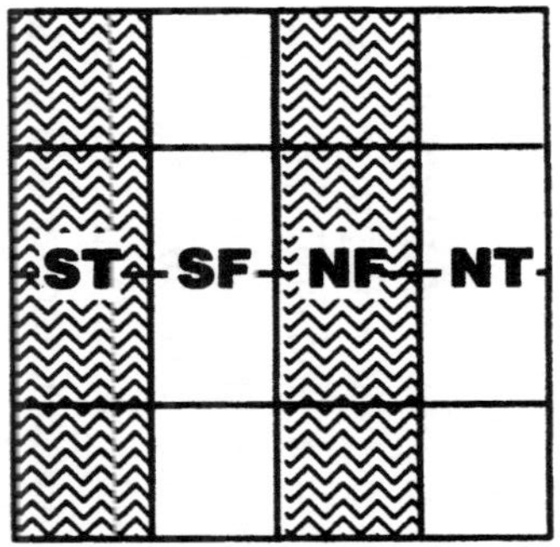

3. Through the Four Columns

Source: *The Type Reporter*, 1985

Intuition learn best through conceptual activities that involve more than one person; Introverts with Intuition learn best through conceptual activities that can be done alone or with one other person.

The Four Temperaments started with the work of David Keirsey (Keirsey, 1989; Keirsey and Bates, 1984). Temperaments cross quadrants and columns, but adherents claim that Sensing/Perception types are playful and clever, Sensing/Judgments are solid and responsible, Intuitive/Thinkings are wise, and Intuitive/Feelings seek to communicate. Those with Sensing/Perception learn through hands-on experience and perform best when given opportunities to construct, operate, or manipulate objects. Those with Sensing/Judgment need to know the practical things; they perform best with programmed learning, worksheets, lecture and recitation, and drill. Those with Intuitive/Thinking deal with abstract matter and collect rules and principles to impose structure upon the knowable world; they perform best with long-term research projects and assignments which call for the collection, clarification, and technical documentation of information. Those with the Intuitive/Feeling temperament use hunches and impressions which are vivid but not detailed; they perform best with small-group processes and role playing.

The Four Columns approach attempts to overlay MBTI upon extant teaching theories rather than devise methods to approach each type, as do the Four Quadrants or the Four Temperaments methods. It also seeks to move people from their strengths to address the "weaknesses" inherent in their types. A teaching approach for those in the Sensing/Feeling column needs to promote self-confidence and use the positive aspects of peer pressure. An approach for those in the Intuitive/Feeling column needs to emphasize creativity and the ability to see old things in new ways. An approach for those in the Intuitive/Thinking column stresses diversity of thought and focus on the process used to reach a conclusion, rather than just upon the conclusion. Those in the Sensing/

Thinking column seem to thrive with a teaching approach where someone else determines what is to be learned, demonstrates it, and then breaks the task down into its smaller parts, allowing the STs to proceed along the task one step at a time.

THE DRAMATIC ART OF INTERNAL MARKETING

Although Grove and Fisk (1992) present a framework for the services experience using theater as a descriptive metaphor which, as the bank story in Chapter 1 shows, has power to clarify, I feel that it does not go far enough in at least two directions. First, by their own admission, Grove and Fisk use this metaphor to describe rather than explain. Second, they view drama and dramaturgy from the outside, as marketers; I had a co-author for a series of articles on this subject who is a published playwright and doctoral student in drama and, thus, views drama and dramaturgy from the inside.

The conventional definition of drama (from the original Greek) is that it means *action*. What action *is* might be defined by what action *does*. To ask "what is the action of the play?" refers not only to physical actions of movement but includes the process of change that occurs within the character(s). The action is illustrated through language and movement. Very simply, action is what happens in a play.

A successful dramatic event combines actions, agents, and intentions in a logical order to make the event understandable to an audience. How to construct successful dramas, then, requires a structure built with believable actions. In part, dramaturgy is the study of dramatic structure. Evaluating how the drama is constructed helps assess its potential understanding. The idea is that if we understand how something is put together, then perhaps we can understand what it means as a whole.

Historically, the structure of plays has followed patterns, not unlike today's prescripted format of television sitcoms and commercial movies. In the *Poetics,* Aristotle (1981) outlined the parts of drama. He observed that all dramas contained six elements: plot, character, thought, diction, music, and spectacle. The latter three refer to the actual production; the former three are contained in the playtext itself. Aristotle also ranked these elements in order of importance, with plot being the most important and spectacle the least. When *Poetics* was rediscovered during the Renaissance, it set off a rash of playwriting activity where everyone tried to write according to Aristotle's rules; today we think of his ideas less as prescriptive than as descriptive categories. Any dramatic situation can be broken down into these six elements. As a tool for assessment, then, Aristotle's system enables us to evaluate strengths and weaknesses of any given situation for its potential to communicate its position.

The traditional and dominant approach to dramatic structure is marked by what Jürgen Habermas (1984) calls "strategic action." Strategic action is action oriented toward exerting an influence. A strategic play tries to convince a reader or audience of its point of view. In other words, the play has the power, because it already knows the answer. The transmission of information is unidirectional. It is not that the play dispenses information with which readers or audiences are unfamiliar; plays strategically oriented serve to remind, reaffirm, and reassert authority, ideologies, and myths within a given cultural context.

Communicative action theory is based upon a belief that people can come together and agree. Whether it is a peace talk, a theater event, or a business meeting, communicative action stresses reaching understanding as its goal, not a passing of information from one party to another.

To communicate is the act of helping someone else understand something. It means that a transference takes place. The basic equation of communication consists of a sender and a receiver with a ratio of one to one. Successful communication occurs when a receiver understands the use of language by a sender in a given circumstance. The art of communication, or transference, is made difficult by a multiplicity of sign systems within the theater context. Semioticians see many sign systems working at the same time: audience, event, action, public, conventions, and the written playtext itself. The art of the theater comprises of the selection and recognition of signifiers placed in a systematic manner. To be successful (i.e., understood), plays rely on constructing conventions that will be recognized by an audience. Language, with its notation system of words and grammatical symbols, is used in plays (written drama) as the predominant link for successful dramatic communication. In performance, dramatic understanding is projected through utterances (verbal and nonverbal). Words are used to imitate human speech as well as to imply actions such as thoughts, emotions, and gestures.

Theater events present complex situations. On a literal level, there are at least four sets of action occurring simultaneously: between characters, between actors, between actor and audience, between actor and character. To complete theater's meta-communication equation, an audience must understand the communication on stage between characters as well as receive the communication offstage from actors. Unlike real-life situations, misunderstanding can be part of successful communication in the theater. Genre structures rely on misunderstandings: comedies are funny because the audience knows the situation while the characters only know a few bits.

On a practical level, misunderstandings in the theater can, and do, occur in the complicated translation process (in this case, writer to director to actor to designer to audience). Depending on the interpretation and timeliness of a play, changes in cultural, social, historical, moral, and ethical codes affect a production's reception. Finally, plays function as blueprints for performance as well as an object to be read. Plays are a construction via language. In order to communicate, the codes must be understandable to the participants involved.

Dramatic understanding of a theater event is possible only if its interpretation is allowed to remain open. If the goal of theater is to communicate an idea or experience in a presentational format, then the success of that communication—or mutual understanding—can be gauged by the agreement made between actor(s) and audience. The point for Habermas (1984) is that this agreement is always negotiable and never stable—much like performance differences due to audience response from night to night. There is no absolutely definitive interpretation; there is no finally definitive production. A drama, regardless of publication history, is never done. What can be is that participants in the communication agree to what is being said and done in the context of the particular time and space of the event. Dramatic understanding is not based upon a prescriptive notion of what is good within a cultural, historical, social, or aesthetic context but rather on a pragmatic assumption that interpretation (and the subsequent judgment) lies somewhere between the writing and the performing of a playtext.

IMPLEMENTATION, NOT THEORY

Truly, we should be at the point in services marketing where we implement what we know, rather than look for new theory. The important point about viewing internal marketing (or indeed, services marketing as a whole) as theater is that the process of so doing leads directly to implementation. Theater is about nothing if it is not about taking a story and making it happen.

Yet the theater metaphor opens the door to something else, something crucial to both a successful services marketing program in general, and an internal marketing program in particular: training the services personnel. Every theatrical performance, no matter how tightly scripted, is unique. It is unique because of differences in the audience, differences in the cast (both in terms of different people and the way each one feels at the time of performance), different settings, etc. If this is as true for services as it is for theater, what are the implications?

First, it makes it more difficult than previously believed to control the behavior and output of the contact person. Mills and Moberg (1990:105) have stated that in order

> "to keep uncertainty within manageable limits, client conduct within the service organization must be monitored and deviations from acceptable behavior minimized. To do this . . . requires a highly detailed view of what forms of client behavior are desired. . . . "

The use of the drama metaphor shows just how difficult a task management faces *even in internal marketing situations where everyone involved is an employee*. If the desire to control behavior becomes obsessive, considerable resources must be devoted to the task of discipline and surveillance "in order to restrict behavioral drift" (Sederberg, 1984). Cahill (1990, 1993), Cahill and Warshawsky (1993, 1995), and Verba and Cahill (1993) describe several attempts to "industrialize the service process" in an attempt to negate some of the problems inherent in the fact that service operations involve people facing people "at the moment of truth." The conclusion of this stream of research is that "industrialization" or "mechanization" through "interactive systems" will not, at least for the near term, get us out of the box that this people-to-people stancc has us in. Technology has, in fact, been called the "service-sector sinkhole" (Hackett, 1990). Although this categorization may seem harsh, the results of the research mentioned above bear out the title. The only practical solution to this problem is to organize the service better and elevate the training of the service providers to a level where they can provide the service desired at a level that the customers desire and with as few operational problems as possible.

Thus, the second implication is that, in the short run at least, the only salvation for a service provider is a good internal marketing program, one which is based upon drama and dramaturgy as the basis of teaching and the organizing metaphor for the training curriculum. What should such a program consist of? At the very least, the internal marketing effort must imbue the organization and its service providers with three crucial understandings. First, no performance will be perfect, no matter how hard the contact person tries; all performances are contingent upon their particular context, and the fact that the service person is following a script does not mean that the customer will follow one. Second, everyone in the organization needs to know everything that is supposed to happen. Third, not every performance is appropriate for every audience. Just as *Oh, Calcutta* should probably not be booked for a performance at a church social, Pranter and Martin (1991) point out that not every customer is appropriate for every service provider because of differences in culture or approach or expectation. Further, they state that it is the firm's responsibility to train their customer contact employees so that they can manage this customer compatibility function, making their employees another market segment (for internal marketing programs to deal with).

No performance follows the script perfectly; whether we are talking about a Shakespeare performance or improvisational comedy. The fact that each performance is staged at the intersection of a live audience, live actors, and live stage hands means that human foibles will enter into the equation, as well as the fact that the emotions of the moment may lead someone to change something in the play. A character may be late getting on stage because of a call of nature or a missed dressing-room call. Someone in the audience may be laughing hysterically at the performance (appropriately or inappropriately–it does not matter). All of these circumstances, and more, lead each performance to differ in some respect or other from all other performances–even from the identical script with the identical cast. And this fact is also true of a well-designed internal marketing program; it must take into consideration the fact that people are involved and people lead to lack of "perfection." Cahill (1992b) addresses a perfect service marketer–Santa Claus; the rest of us must be satisfied with something less, and design our programs and training accordingly.

Given the intangible nature of services, given the fact that each provider can be viewed as a division of the firm, internal marketing in particular, and services marketing in general, are subject to all of the difficulties of managing decentralized organizations. Jay (1967:65) tells of St. Augustine's only rule for Christian conduct: "Love God and do as you like." The implication, of course, is that if you truly love God, you will like to do only the things that God will find pleasing. This is the essence of the training for internal marketing purposes; people must be deeply inculcated with what the firm really wants and believes (steeped in the corporate culture, speaking the language that may be peculiar to the firm [Miller, 1987], in other words) before they can be trusted to act properly. Close supervision and technological scrutiny will not work, certainly not in the long term. Without respect at the point of providing the service, respect for the employee, and respect for the customer, everything falls apart (Bitran and Hoech, 1990). And it is at this point that the concern of Rafiq and Ahmed (1993) mentioned previously, the concern that internal marketing seems to be an attempt to usurp human resources management, can be laid to rest. Human resources management is about people information; internal marketing is about service information. Both are necessary to the good functioning of a service firm.

Internal marketing may not necessarily be about "empowerment," but a drama focus would require it to be about empowerment. In fact, a drama focus shows that services marketing in general, and internal marketing in particular, is truly improvisational theater. Goldberg (1991) defines four basic rules for improvisational comedy which also apply to internal marketing programs: Don't Deny; Show Us, Don't Tell Us; Play the Moment;

and Play the Scene Legitimately. "Don't Deny" simply means that one has to accept the information that has gone before; this is quite true when there is no tangible product to fall back upon, when information is everything. "Show Us, Don't Tell Us" concerns the service encounter when the service is performed, without a lengthy discussion of how it will be done. Once the sale is made and the service is to be performed, it behooves the contact person to simply perform it. "Play the Moment" is where empowerment starts. In order to "Play the Moment," people will require information–the more information the better. Information (staying in the drama metaphor) about one's character, about what situation one is in, and what does the character and the others in the scene want, etc. Management has to have faith in its personnel so that it can do what needs to be done at that moment; although it may appear that this facet of services marketing management may be better described as customer service management, it is probable that if more attention were devoted to "playing the moment" at the point of providing the service, less attention would be needed for customer service. "Play the Scene Legitimately" simply means staying in character. All of these aspects of improvisational comedy seem to apply directly to internal marketing; not that marketing is funny (comedy often is not, either), but the improvisatory nature of internal marketing is clear.

However, the part of improvisational comedy that has the clearest impact upon internal marketing is that improvisational theater requires the entire troupe to know everyone else in the troupe well enough to be able to play a scene to the strengths of each other member. They need to have worked with each other for some time, have rehearsed and done other improvisational work–both practice and real–so that they are aware of each other at a level that non-thespians can only approximate without extensive training and practice in similar techniques. Internal marketing requires extensive training with many techniques; it truly is a case of "Love God and do what you like."

Chapter 5

Innovation?

WHY INNOVATION?

Most Americans are familiar with the following quotation (or at least the part of it about building mousetraps), even if we are unaware that it is attributed to Ralph Waldo Emerson:

> If a man write a better book, preach a better sermon, or make a better mouse-trap than his neighbor, tho' he build his house in the woods, the world will make a beaten path to his door.

Our society praises innovation and invention. Academics state that entrepreneurial careers can be lengthened by innovation and serially founding new enterprises (Ronstadt, 1988); other academics have reported at length upon the extension of firms' lives by programs of ongoing innovation (Jelinek and Schoonhoven, 1993).

Trudel (1994) tells the tale of one of the first assignments undertaken by his firm, which was to help a "quintessential technology venture: very technocentric, with an innovative but eccentric founder." Its product (which Trudel with unintended irony calls its "better mousetrap") was "both clever and cute," had good early sales, but the sales level never approached the "hockey-stick" curve which the company wanted. Trudel did some research, including talking to people who had bought the product. He told one customer, "I don't see how you can use this product." The customer confessed, "I can't, but I like it anyway." Trudel's conclusion was that the product was useless; however, the engineers were "irritated" that their marketing minions were not performing–a classic example of Emersonian innovation. Trudel states that "too many high-tech firms are bringing out overhyped products that sell well to the lunatic fringe, but then peter out because the product doesn't fill a real need for the rest of us" (Trudel, 1994; see also Cahill and Warshawsky [1993] for a further discussion of this problem).

I have consulted with dozens of entrepreneurs, almost all of whom have articulated this Emersonian paradigm with respect to their enterprise or product. They have a "perfect" product or service in mind; if they can only sell it to "one percent of the people who need it," they will be rich. No research, no marketing will be needed–just a story on the news and "the world will beat a path to my door." Not one of these enterprises has matched expectations in this regard.

Everett Rogers, a leading authority on innovation, defines an innovation as an "idea, practice, or object that is perceived as new by an individual or another unit of adoption. An innovation presents an individual or an organization with a new alternative or alternatives, with new means of solving problems" (Rogers, 1983:xviii-xix). But the probabilities of the innovation's being superior to the old way are not known, so people must seek information on the innovation in order to cope with its uncertainty. The *Webster's New World Dictionary* (1964:753) has a simpler, more concise, definition: "something newly introduced; new method, custom, device, etc.; change in the way of doing things."

Innovation, although it is inextricably linked with creativity, is not the same thing as creativity. Creativity is the process of identifying either a problem that was previously unrecognized or a solution that is novel or outside the experience of others (Edwards and Sproull, 1984). According to Dauw (1969:85), innovation is an organizational or social process that *follows* invention–"the product of an original, elaborating, highly creative thinker who can usually germinate novel ideas rather fluently"–which is highly personal. Smith (1993) has developed a seven-level process to link creativity and innovation: Do things right, do the right things, do away with things, do things better, do things other people are doing, do things that have not been done, do things that cannot be done.

HOW MUCH INNOVATION?

There are many opportunities for or constraints upon the innovation process; however, they may be categorized into two overarching groupings: Environmental and Internal to the firm (United States Department of Commerce, 1983:67-68).

Environmental factors consist of:

- the technological base
- overall economic conditions
- price stability
- industry composition
- government policies
- research and Development incentives

Although these environmental factors are important to the success of any innovation effort, this is a book on internal marketing, not innovation. (For those with more interest in the innovation process itself, there is an enormous literature; see also Cahill [1993] for a further development of these environmental factors as they impact upon innovation in professional services firms.)

Factors internal to the corporation consist of:

- corporate goals
- corporate financial profile
- managerial quality

Corporate goals–setting the desired rate of return from projects, desired market share for products or services offered, desired rates of growth, etc.–drive a firm's day-to-day operational decisions about new products or services. For example, if desired rates of return are high, coupled with a short payback period, it would be difficult to justify many new projects.

The corporate financial profile can be crucial to the firm's ability to develop new products or services, place new plants and equipment into service, or seek to expand market share. If a firm has a high degree of debt acquired as a part of a leveraged buyout, that could hamper management's short-term ability to add new products or services (Fox and Marcus, 1992). If a firm has good positive cash flow, on the other hand, "buying" market share with new projects may be feasible.

Managerial quality, on the other hand, is more difficult to analyze objectively, especially from outside the firm. The level of management's understanding of the technological base of the industry, for example, may preclude a firm's entrance into a long-term research and development project if the management personnel have only recently come from a different industry with different technological needs. But vastly outweighing this management characteristic is management's overall comfort with risk. Innovation is, by definition, fraught with risk. Can a firm's management stand the heat? Can it adequately reward the people on whom it depends for developing the innovation without, on the one hand straining the firm's system of rewards and punishments, nor on the other hand turning the development "team" into disgruntled ex-employees who will immediately set up a competing firm? Can it kill a project that has only limited chances of success before the project turns into a resource drain?

Efforts to deinstitutionalize a project in an entrepreneurial-oriented company when initiated by those other than the entrepreneur or shareholders will probably cause management to proceed more forcefully with the losing project. Examples of this trend are legion in the recent past. The only way that this dilemma seems to be resolved is if the outsiders–be they employees, lenders, etc.–can get enough leverage to force the entrepreneur to the sidelines and salvage the firm–often at the expense of the losing project. Steven Jobs at Apple Computer and Edwin Land at Polaroid are classic examples. Likewise, changing the reality of a project's economics in an entrepreneurial firm will mean little without changing the psychology of the project for the entrepreneur.

New firms have no organization history or experience; founders of those firms tend to have unbalanced experience. In a sense, then, the history of any successful entrepreneurial venture is a history of escalation. Thus, innovation only causes escalation problems when the project does not come in on time and on budget. The more experience a firm or an entrepreneur has with successful innovation, even innovation unrelated to the current project, the more likely it will be that escalation/exit difficulties will occur when a project is delayed or has cost overruns. Ronstadt (1988) discusses the importancc to entrepreneurs' careers of venturing afield from even their entrepreneurial experience. As business success piles upon earlier personal success, the ability diminishes to "pull the plug" quickly.

INNOVATION VERSUS COMPETENCE

Newness of services–innovation itself–leads to quality that is irregular or even bad in the service provided. It takes time for professionals to digest new laws or regulations or methods of solving client problems. During the time when this digestion is taking place, it is possible–indeed, even probable–that some clients will get advice or documents which are incorrect or certainly unclear. After the time necessary for reflection and internalizing changes has passed, uniformity in documents and advice will again occur. However, the transition period will be fraught with danger for the client–and, ultimately, for the provider as well, who will need to ascertain which clients have not been well served during the interregnum.

There are risks to users and providers alike caused by the failure of the service, no matter what the cause of that failure. These risks are of two major categories: reputation and financial. The risk to reputation because of a service failure can be at least as damaging as the direct financial impact, since providers have little to differentiate themselves from the competition and little to offer clients or potential clients save their reputation. A law firm that is fined by regulators for violation of ethics canons or regulatory procedures will find it more difficult to convince prospects that their work will be properly handled by the firm. Thus the firm faces the possibility of losing existing clients who are concerned that their reputations may be tainted by association. Consider this example: a client is listed in the paper as subject to an audit or penalty from an audit because of work which was improperly performed by its accounting firm. Even if the client does not sue, a certain chill is likely to invade the relationship. A client of the author's had to file an amended tax return less than two weeks after the original return had been filed because of the failure of his accountant to include $250,000 in rental income on the personal return that the same accountant had deducted as rental expense on the corporate return. Then the accountant sent the client a bill for preparing and filing the amended return. In the end, of course, the accountant rescinded the bill. Needless to say, however, the relationship between my client and his accountant was soured and, although the client still retains this accounting firm, the relationship has never returned to its former warmth.

Jelinek and Schoonhoven (1993) undertook a long-term study of the innovation process in five firms in the integrated circuit industry, which they insist on calling the "electronics industry": Texas Instruments, Hewlett-Packard, National Semiconductor, Intel, and Motorola. Its focus is firmly upon innovation management within the firm. Why this focus and this industry? The authors state unequivocally that the model of the electronics industry is the model for future competitiveness: constant change, short production runs which do not allow for much in the way of "learning curve" effects, and frequent new products.

When they embarked on the research, Jelinek and Schoonhoven expected—as most researchers probably would have—that the Burns and Stalker (1961) formula of organic organizations (ambiguous reporting relations, unclear job responsibilities, consultative decision making, and lateral communication patterns) would be what they found in their sample of successful innovators. Instead, they found organizations that had very clear job responsibilities, and extremely unambiguous reporting relations—in short, modified hierarchies. One reason for this, they are quick to point out, is the fact that their sample consists of very large organizations with thousands of employees and billions of dollars in sales that would probably collapse if they were organized any other way. Thus, Jelinek and Schoonhoven have conflated two separate ideas—economic foundations and organizational style—that are generally conflated in peoples' minds. How do these organizations successfully fly in the teeth of innovation folklore that maintains only the small can innovate and that hierarchies are death to anything smacking of the new?

First, managements have successfully balanced change and stability within their firms—stability in areas that do not need to change, change where it is necessary. This tension between change and stability is reflected in these firms' frequent reorganizations; when the hierarchy cannot be fine-tuned for a better result, it must be totally remachined.

Second, despite their enormous size, these firms have managed to preserve a "small company" culture. For instance, many of their interviewees frequently reiterated stories of founders of their firm, or long-term managers, even though in some instances these individuals were long dead.

Third, these firms are engineer-driven and there is apparent relish on the part of many of the employees inherent in staying at the cutting edge of technology, with all of the risk implicit in being there. This fact also leads to the fourth point–the "traditional" hierarchies are attacked (but only by the engineers and scientists) and not by others in the organization. They are attacked because these firms have made it possible for people with ideas to get them to others in the firm without necessarily having to go up the chain of command for a decision.

Fifth, all of these firms have explicit innovation goals that include market success. In every one of the firms in their sample, the innovators measure their success not by "how good it is," but rather by how well it sells.

And here is some hope for making it possible for service firms to innovate successfully. There seem to be three direct avenues out of the dilemma, not necessarily mutually exclusive, and one basic mindset that can make it all possible. The avenues are the use of unconditional service guarantees, a reduction in innovation itself, and the use of an expert-system approach to the problem. The basic mindset is the use of internal marketing in many forms to make it all work.

GUARANTEES

Unconditional service guarantees as they apply to existing services have already been thoroughly discussed in Chapter 2. In terms of service innovations, however, they help market innovations by eliminating what computer people call the "FUD Factor"–Fear, Uncertainty, and Doubt. Services cannot be test driven before they are bought, so there is a high perceived risk factor in using a service innovation. Many services can be used only once and not returned after use. Once a will is written by the lawyer, the service has been used up. A consultant's recommendations that do not work out cannot be returned to the consultant. In mid-1994, Figgie International, Incorporated, a troubled conglomerate, sued the Boston Consulting Group for at least $2 million, charging that the firm provided "erroneous" market studies and "flawed" strategies (Narisetti, 1994) and later in the year sued Deloitte and Touche for at least $250 million charging the consulting firm provided services that have "proven essentially worthless"–in return for some $55 million in fees, of which Figgie paid $22 million (and for the balance of which Deloitte and Touche has filed suit) (Solov, 1994). Filing suit against a consultant is quite rare, and consultants have rarely been held responsible for their recommendations. This is a ghastly state of affairs; Jeffrey Sonnenfeld of Emory University is quoted in Narisetti (1994:B1) as stating that "any embers that suggest there could be a spreading flame of enthusiasm for making consulting firms accountable will be a very good thing; [why] nobody has challenged the quality of consultants' data before is extraordinary." Nevertheless, the import of this suit is clear, whether Figgie prevails or not: There is at least an implied guarantee given by service providers to their clients, whether that guarantee is explicit or not. This should lead consultants to be more careful in their engagements, and perhaps seek contracts to implement their recommendations–for it is all too easy for the consultant to claim that it was not the recommendation that was wrong, but rather the implementation by the client that was flawed. Sometimes, the consultant is correct in that diagnosis.

Yet most people cannot imagine a higher risk than an Internal Revenue Service audit caused by a "bad" tax return, or the chaos in one's estate caused by a "bad" will. Guarantees can do two things for the innovating organization, if properly put into place. First, they can serve notice to the service providers in the organization that there are standards of service that must be met–a component of a good internal marketing program. Second, unconditional service guarantees can focus the attention of the organization on areas of its business where service innovations have a major impact–another portion of a good internal marketing program.

REDUCING INNOVATION

A second avenue out of the dilemma seems to be for the firm to simply reduce innovativeness. Although this avenue seems to fly in the face of advice, particularly from the practitioner arena, to "increase competitiveness through innovativeness," the drive for increased innovation has real problems for clients and providers alike, which have been outlined above. Perhaps simply reducing the number of new ideas which a firm will consider might help to stabilize the delivery of quality services to clients. After all, in many service experiences, demand for the service is not truly driven by the client; rather it is "environmentally driven." How many audited corporate financial statements would be produced in the absence of a requirement that all publicly held corporations present audited financial statements annually to their shareholders? How many times would individuals have their wills re-written in the absence of changes in the federal income tax and estate tax laws? How often would a consulting firm be able to sell its services to clients for ideas that *it* had for a client rather than respond to a request by a potential client that the firm help with the client's ideas?

There is a story, unfortunately probably apocryphal, about a county extension agent–fresh out of the state agricultural college–who was driving on a remote back road. He saw an old farmer who was using antiquated techniques and equipment, the type that his professors had railed against repeatedly, holding up this type of farmer as an exemplar of the very person who the extension agent should try to reform. Well, the extension agent got out of his car and tried to reform this old farmer. Finally, the old man had had enough. He took his hat off, spit tobacco in the general direction of the young man's shoes, scratched himself in several places and said, "Tell you what, sonny; everything you say might be right. Probably is, what with you've been to college and all. But, hell, boy, I already don't farm near as good as I know how." If, for whatever reason, this approach seems to be inappropriate for a particular firm, perhaps reducing its innovativeness to finding new ways of producing and delivering the firm's existing services will achieve the same end. If demand for most professional services is environmental in nature, innovative *delivery systems* will allow firms to differentiate themselves from their competition *while providing essentially identical offerings* and lowering the risks of innovativeness to both the providers and their clients.

EXPERT SYSTEMS

A third avenue is to use "expert systems" to devise a path to meaningful and restrained innovation that is in the best interests of clients and providers alike. Expert systems are computer programs that distill the mastery of one or more "experts" in a field so that the program can simulate the actions of the expert when faced with the particular circumstances for which it is designed. These systems are just beginning to come to prominence in several fields, including services (Burke et al., 1988; Cahill, 1990; Wiesendanger, 1991). Expert systems seem to work by the systematic application of the expert's knowledge–something that experts are often incapable of doing. It is a truism (again, alas, possibly apocryphal) in the field that expert systems frequently outperform the experts–even the experts whose expertise was used to construct the system. The reason for this outperforming by the software is explained by the fact that its expertise is applied *systematically.*

How is the concept of expert systems applicable to innovation for service firms? Simply put, a system could be built utilizing the best knowledge about successful innovation practices and their application. Although there is little published on the field of service innovation, there is a wealth of information on innovation and innovativeness, creativity, adoption of innovation, and similar topics spread across many disciplines such as marketing, education, and sociology. A transdiscipline team could be assembled to create this expert system to be developed to allow service firms to weed out the innovations that would be problematic for the firm to adopt or troublesome in operation for the client. If properly designed and implemented, such a system should produce fewer but better innovations which could be adopted with less concern over the FUD factor by clients and firms alike. Gupta and Rogers (1991) recommend formalizing the integration of marketing and research and development–in other words, nonautomated expert systems–to help implementation of innovations, as well as that firms should develop internal change agents to improve the whole innovation process.

ROLE OF INTERNAL MARKETING IN INNOVATION PROCESS

Now, what does all of this have to do with internal marketing? Simply put, the proper application of the Marketing Concept through a well-designed internal marketing program can reduce the risks of innovation to the firm and to its customers. Despite the research focus in the integrated circuit industry, Jelinek and Schoonhoven's book can shed some light on how this can be done. Their third point–that the firms they researched are engineer driven and there is apparent relish on the part of many of the employees inherent in staying at the cutting edge of technology–can be translated into "professional driven." And their fifth point–that all of the firms have explicit innovation goals that include *market success* and that in every one of the firms in their sample the innovators measure their success by how well it sells–are crucial.

Table 5.1 presents a list of factors associated with successful innovation in computer software. Some of the factors are simply restatements of the Marketing Concept; others represent the operation of an internal marketing program. Innovation forces a firm to stand with two marketing faces in two different directions, a particularly crucial stance for service providers. The first direction is, of course, outward to the external market. What do customers want? How badly? Are they willing to pay for what they want? How much? These are the standard questions that new-product researchers (and new-service researchers in recent years) are used to dealing with.

It is the internal direction that is relatively new. Jelinek and Schoonhoven found, however, that the best innovators in their sample practiced what can only be described as internal marketing (but the engineers at these firms would never call it that). They quote (1993:76-77) Jim Feibiger from Motorola about how the problem-solving process worked there. Explicit aims include practicality, support, and resources, along with managerial attention, insistence on results, and specific responsibility. This was "accomplished by bringing the needed expertise and the responsible decision makers together in the same room at the same time" and insisting that everything be taken care of at the moment when everyone is together.

Other firms do things a bit differently. Some expect employees to "steal" time and other resources from their assigned jobs to develop products and services to the point where they can become officially sanctioned projects. Other firms require that someone with a new product idea "sell" it to another employee; this approach has worked well at Hewlett-Packard. The basis of this approach is that if another employee cannot see any use for your innovation, it is unlikely that an outside customer would, either. This approach seems to be relatively easy to establish for products, especially the testing equipment with which Hewlett-Packard has established its reputation. It is probably not so directly applicable for services, although there are undoubtedly some service applications for which it would work and work well. But as Rhyne (1993, 1994) states in concluding his articles

TABLE 5.1. Success Factors Associated with Successful Innovation

1. Recognizing user needs.
2. Good communication by the innovator.
3. Good management of technical aspects.
4. Presence of a product champion with status.
5. Availability of adequate resources.
6. Good marketing.
7. Planned innovation as a corporate policy.
8. Good management practice in the innovation process.

Source: Voss (1985), pp. 124-125. These are listed in descending order of frequency of mention in the research reported in the Voss article.

about the impact of the management of innovative design on the America's Cup competition, companies who wish to innovate and do it well need to focus on developing teams that will function together over time, recognize the need for continuous improvement over time, and recognize that experience in the industry remains critical. This sounds very much like it would apply to internal marketing situations.

Services, particularly professional services, are often never used. I am currently on my third will; the first two were, obviously, not used. When the tax laws change again, I suppose that I will have to go in for will number four. Although this is clearly not the fault of my attorney, I am not happy to have to pay him to prepare a revision of my will that was caused by no change in my personal circumstances. And, of course, I have no idea how well-written the will is; a will is the quintessential "single-use" item. If it is poorly drawn, there is no hope for improvement the next time, "doing the service very right the second time." But wills are not the only "one-offs"; my consulting engagements are almost totally project-based rather than ongoing relationships. I only have one chance to give the correct advice.

A will is also a good example to use for the wide temporal

separation between the "production" of a service and its "use" that can occur with professional services. We are so conditioned by thinking of services as inseparable and intangible that we forget that the service produced–the will–is only part of the total service. Until the person for whom the will is drawn dies and the estate is probated under the terms of that will, *the service is not complete*. Three years may elapse between the time an accountant files a tax return for an individual or corporation and the Internal Revenue Service conducts a review or an audit; until that lapse of time, *the service is not complete*. This temporal separation of parts of the service raises the level of risk, certainly in the client's perception, for the client.

Nevertheless, a good lawyer will be able to critique an innovation in will writing presented by another lawyer; a good accountant will be able to critique a financial procedure devised by another accountant. This fact is the important part of Jelinek and Schoonhoven's statement of Hewlett-Packard's insistence on selling "to the next bench." It is also this fact which informs the peer-review process, whether one is discussing medical regulation or scholarly journal publishing. The internal "customers" cannot replace the outside market unless the product or service is primarily intended for internal use, but they can screen ideas before they become catastrophic drains on corporate resources with no hope of ever attaining market success.

The use of internal marketing as an innovation screening device requires an ongoing commitment by management to keep employees at the cutting edge of developments both in the industry and the employees' fields of expertise far beyond that needed to perform their job competently–another example of "beyond competence." A solid grounding in new techniques; a wide acquaintance with the research literature in the field (where applicable, and it is more applicable than management in many industries cares to admit); a wide acquaintance with leaders in the field that can be developed only through meeting and interacting with these leaders at workshops, conferences, and meetings; a deep familiarity with customers and their needs developed through long acquaintance with them and their plants and facilities developed through a series of customer visits (McQuarrie, 1993)–all of these parts of an internal marketing program will help to screen innovations, allowing the firm to keep the good ones and throw away those which seem to have less chance of market success.

What role can a series of customer visits play in an *internal* marketing program? The type of customer visit program described by McQuarrie (1993:36) is a systematic, qualitative research tool designed to elicit responses to:

- identifying new product opportunities;
- identifying new market opportunities;
- exploring customer likes and dislikes in current offerings;
- exposing customer perceptions of intangibles;
- describing the role played by the product in the customer's operation;
- describing the customer's decision model and process for choosing among vendors.

Further, this program is not just a case of sending out the marketing vice president with some of the sales force to see their "good" customers; it is a research tool that McQuarrie envisions will be used by many employees across an organization at various levels and will allow them to communicate with the rest of the organization. Thus it will fulfill some of the criteria mentioned above about customer contact and deeper technical knowledge. A well-designed internal marketing program will allow good employees from various levels to interact well as a team, vastly increasing the probable success of this type of customer visitation program.

Thus, internal marketing coupled with an understanding implementation of the Marketing Concept as a gatekeeper to the firm's innovation efforts can play a vital role in reducing the potential costs of new product and service failure. And these costs can be staggering, far outweighing the additional costs of the specific aspects of an innovation-screening internal marketing program mentioned above.

Chapter 6

What Have We Gained?

I keep a log of both good and bad service encounters to use as examples in teaching and in my consulting practice. I would like to share three encounters as case examples for enumerating some lessons in a too-frequent customer-services/marketing problem. The problem seems to me not to have improved much over the past few years, despite all the articles, television programs, and seminars to which so many of us have been subjected that have attempted to alleviate it.

THE HOSPITAL

My wife recently went to a local hospital for a "routine" mammogram. First, she had to wait, despite having made an appointment; in order to pass the time, she picked up a copy of the hospital's newsletter. On page three was a correction to an article in the previous quarter's issue about diet during sieges of PMS. My wife has lately undergone a prescribed dietary change, so suddenly she is interested in articles relating to diet. The correction indicated that the information about carbohydrate/protein ratios in the previous article was incorrect; my wife tried to find a copy of that issue to read what it had said. (Chances are we received the newsletter at home; we get at least six newsletters from local hospitals, but who looks at those things intently?) The hospital could not locate a copy of the errant newsletter, nor even a photocopy of the offending article. This is hardly calculated to delight a patient, but this is often a problem with printing corrections in subsequent editions.

Then, mammogram complete, my wife had the temerity to ask about results, knowing that the hospital did not provide them. A competing hospital advertises that "flash" results will be ready before you leave and the radiologist will call the next day with a complete report. "We don't do that; 'flash' reports are not reliable. Results will be available in five to seven days." Delightful? Competitive? And yet this hospital *knows* that its competition is advertising speedy results, which is what everyone who has any kind of examination wants. It was at this point that the journal-reviewer mentioned in the Preface stated that my wife's doctor should have explained the hospital's policy about releasing results; my wife *knew* the hospital's policy and simply was attempting to lodge a protest to that policy as a customer. A protest should have been unnecessary; if the hospital had addressed its competitive position (it has done so with respect to another hospital in town with drastic results), it might have reached another conclusion. Even if it had not, it would not have seemed quite so clinical and detached about the concern that its patients have toward the results of mammograms.

To end this list of lack of customer-centered activities a card was handed to my wife when she left. On it was an explanation of why her breasts may be sore–*and a list of things she should do before her next mammogram* (which may be years in the future), *some of which require her to schedule the mammography within her menstrual cycle*. This information obviously should have been conveyed to her before *this* examination to allow her to schedule the examination to minimize discomfort. This is where the doctor should have been involved–to hand this card to his patient when he told her to make an appointment for a mammogram–if the hospital radiology department cannot be trusted to perform this simple task over the telephone. The hospital failed totally to delight its customer no matter how hard all of us in the fields of services marketing and customer service have worked to get service providers to do so routinely (Cahill, 1992a, 1992b). Worse, it probably has lost at least one patient because of this process, as my wife has indicated that she might use the competition next time. And we certainly mention the above episode when friends ask us about mammography and where to go for the service.

THE AUTO CLUB

My car died in the fall while I was picking up my son from nursery school. I called the Auto Club, was told the truck would be along "sometime" within 45 minutes, and I should wait by my car; the truck arrived in ten minutes. The car needed to be towed to a garage, which it was. The tow truck driver was kind enough to drop my son and me at home, about a mile from the garage. No charge for the tow–a service included in the membership fee–no charge for the "cab ride" home–not included in the membership fee, but an extra provided by a kind tow truck operator for which his employer would not be reimbursed. The Auto Club-approved garage fixed what was wrong–a broken timing belt–and sent me on my way the next day after paying $250.

Two days later my car died again; this time it was late in the evening, so I did not call the Auto Club until the next morning–from home, since there was no convenient public phone near my car. I spoke to an operator who told me: only the first three miles of towing was free (this was news to me–I had not been told that earlier in the week), that I needed to be at the car to be towed (this has never happened to me before), if I was not at the car the driver would wait five minutes and then leave–billing me for a service call–and because I was 20 minutes away from where my car was stuck I was going to have a problem, as she would not hold my call but would immediately put it into the system, and calls were being picked up within ten minutes.

I asked for her supervisor, who picked up the phone after about a two-minute delay. She never identified herself as a supervisor and simply repeated everything the operator had told me with no elaboration. When I attempted to move the conversation away from the script she was obviously following, such as mentioning that I had been a dues-paying member of the club for 18 years, it had no effect. There was no conversation, only a regurgitation of rote-learned SOP (Standard Operating Procedure). There was no attempt on the part of the supervisor (who, for all I know, was only another operator pretending to be a supervisor) to address the problems that a club member was having with the service or with the operator who originally took the call. Subsequently, during the terribly cold weather we had that winter, several cars were towed from my neighborhood when their owners were nowhere near the vicinity of the car by individuals who had called the Auto Club to have the car towed.

THE RETAIL OPERATION

A colleague who is a computer system integrator and who does over $100,000 of business annually with a local computer store was recently informed that, because of the inconvenience it had caused its customers by moving, the store was going to give them a $25 rebate on their next purchase. Delighted, because *he* had not felt inconvenienced by their move, my colleague deducted $25 from his next bill from them, representing over $5,000 of purchases. He spent the next two months being dunned by their collections department because he applied the $25 to his next purchase–as the store's letter had indicated–instead of waiting for a coupon to be applied to the purchase after that, which the store was planning to send out "Real Soon Now." When he read the store's offering letter to the collection person, it made no impression. He dealt with his salesperson, who got nowhere with his management. My colleague is now doing business with another store, and the first store has lost over $100,000 per year over a misinterpretation of a $25 offer, *which was supposed to make customers happy* because of a previous inconvenience. What is going on here? Why are we still here?

Three incidents out of my log. What do they have in common? I am afraid that these examples have all too much in common. It has been several years since the outpouring of books and articles on services marketing started (Shanks, 1985; Hart, 1988; Heskett, Sasser, and Hart, 1990; Berry and Parasuraman, 1991). We certainly should know how to market services, how to please service customers, and how to do our jobs as service providers correctly. Why these examples? I believe that we *do* know how to do the job correctly. Then why are we *not* doing the job correctly? Simply put, too many companies do not want to do the job correctly because they perceive–incorrectly in most cases–that it is too expensive for them to change their well-known, time-honored, tried-and-true (but incorrect) old ways.

Two reviewers of an early draft of an article covering material similar to this complained that I had ignored the theory of services marketing. One reviewer even directed me to a favorite author of his, but then stated that not citing more of the theoretical material would "damage the author's hook–citations of poor service." I believe that these reviewers missed the point. It is clear to me that we *know* how to provide superior service, not just in theory but in practice. We should be far past the time of theory generation in services marketing and deeply into the implementation phase. As I see it, however, the problem concerns management's failure to do what we know needs to be done to provide superior service. The three stories cited above clearly show this. What is wrong?

1. All too often, as in the case of the Auto Club example–and countless other examples–firms are still hiring based on the traditional retail-industry model of paying the lowest possible wages and accepting the inevitable employee turnover (as well as

customers disgruntled by these underpaid and undertrained employees) as part of the cost of doing business. I have noted an upsurge of this mentality as the economy has gotten worse and more people are looking for work. Instead of hiring qualified people who will stay with an employer for a long period of time if properly trained and paid, too many employers are trying to save a nickel by hiring at minimum wage and handing out scripts or operating manuals and not caring about the customer. We know better than this; we have had years of being told not to do this. Frederick Hertzberg (1973) taught us how to motivate employees (and it was not with money, which he considered to be a "hygiene factor"–one whose absence was a dismotivator, but whose presence was not motivating). My stories are hardly unique. Why should today be any different from when the economy was better? I have a client who has recently started an inbound/outbound telemarketing operation. She is paying better-than-prevailing wages in her area–plus generous bonuses and commissions when she can get them from her customers (and small ones herself when she cannot get them from her customers). She trains her operators on each product or service they are selling, will not allow them to use scripts, and is doing well. From the first month of operation, her firm has been profitable. It can be done. All it takes is the willingness to spend some money on training and reinforcement of the desired behaviors.

2. There is too much focus on the organization itself. This is the result, primarily, of the "Total Quality Movement," which focuses the firm's attention in on itself instead of outward toward the market and the customer. This kind of attention is glaringly obvious in the example of the Hospital case. It may possibly be true that "flash" mammogram reports are not as reliable as traditional reviews; I cannot say. But whether they are or not is not an important issue. The important issue is that the hospital was clearly more concerned with *its* needs than those of its customers, most of whom want to hear right away that their mammo-

grams were "clean," instead of waiting in an agony of suspense for five to seven days. If one hospital is willing to stake its reputation on providing flash reports available and making the advertising of this service its *key differentiation strategy in a terribly crowded market,* should my wife's hospital not at least look into why such a strategy is being followed? Is it possible that a 90 percent accuracy factor, but instant results, is better than a 98 percent accuracy factor involving and agonizing waiting period? TQM would say no, but TQM tends to be run by an engineering mentality, one that is not truly concerned with what the customer wants. TQM never focuses on being only good enough for what the customer is concerned about and will pay for; it insists on "6-Sigma Quality" or some such, when no customer beyond an engineer cares, or even knows what one Sigma might be. Lest there be any misinterpretation on this point, I am not in favor of "Quality Management"–it is anti-customer; it is internally focused.

3. Making life difficult for the customer but easier for the organization continues to be a way of life in too many organizations. This is the essence of the Retail Operation case. It makes a difference to sales, obviously, if my rebate for your inconvenience is $25 off your current bill or a $25 coupon on your next purchase. It has been seven years since Christopher Hart's article (1988) addressed the need for service guarantees as a marketing device. One of the clear points in that article was that guarantees need to be easy for the customer to call the organization on. I had a newspaper client who, several years ago offered a money-back guarantee on advertisement mistakes that required people to find the office (difficult), come in between 3 and 5 p.m. on Friday and accept a check. My client's manager prided himself on almost never paying on the guarantee, despite the fact that the firm frequently made mistakes in advertising copy. This attitude can no longer be tolerated, yet managements not only tolerate it but in many cases encourage it.

4. An attitude of "the customer is an idiot" or "the customer has nowhere else to go" pervades too many organizations today. This is one of the problems in the Auto Club case. The Auto Club has a captive market: I've paid my dues, so I'm stuck. During this past winter, it was impossible to get a garage to come jump a car unless you were a member of the Auto Club, because all of their crews were busy with Auto Club business.

Make no mistake, this is a management problem, not an employee problem. Systems have to be put in place to allow employees to act in ways which they as people would act and to allow them to treat customers as they would wish to be treated if they were the organization's customers. (For instance, keeping copies of past newsletters on file at all patient contact points is essential. Newspapers learned this lesson decades ago; if one prints retractions or corrections, people will want to see the original story.)

Hoffman and Ingram (1992) report the result of a survey of 250 home healthcare professionals asking people to rate themselves on such statements as "I try to help clients achieve their goals," "I try to achieve my goals by satisfying clients," and similar basic customer service themes. Their findings showed that the overall job satisfaction of the healthcare workers–as well as their satisfaction with work, co-workers, supervisors, and promotion–was positively correlated, not with their pay, but with their customer orientation, which the authors define as "the practice of the marketing concept at the level of the individual service provider and customer" (Hoffman and Ingram, 1992:69).

CUSTOMER SERVICE

How does an organization implement superior customer service? Or, perhaps more to the point, what today should be considered "good" customer service–that is, delighting the customer? The Marketing Concept will do fine. Not difficult in theory, but obviously–based upon three of the incidents from my log and the hundreds of war stories I have heard down through the years—not easy in practice. The organization must be reorganized around this notion that the customer and his or her wants are paramount to the organization. Is this not internal marketing? This cannot mean saving a few cents on the hourly wage of telephone service representatives or other front-line service personnel if by so doing the organization hires mediocre talent. The sales lost because of customers disgruntled by these employees will far outweigh the few cents saved. We all know this. What needs to be done is to develop a simple implementation model that will convince managements to execute a competent, properly designed customer service program.

Customer service is, of course, the front line, the trenches, the "moment of truth" writ large. Any help that can be provided to those employees who spend their time working with customers, often not overly happy with the organization or with being in contact with the organization's personnel, has to serve to better the application of the organization's mission. I believe that it is at this point that a particularly appropriate application of drama as metaphor and organizing vision as mentioned in Chapter 4 becomes useable.

Services marketing theorists are notorious for advocating a strategy of getting the customers involved with providing the service. Many kinds of services cannot be provided without the live participation of the customer; these services run a gamut from will preparation to attendance at an amusement park. Or a theatrical performance. If services marketers wish to increase the participation of the users, how apt the drama metaphor becomes!

But why should the customer participate in the delivery of a service? Part of the attraction of hiring others to perform a service is the possibility of lying back and relaxing while someone else does the work, right? When I go to the grocery store, one that still hires baggers, I frequently do my own bagging, primarily to get out of the store faster, but also to get things bagged the way I like them. I am always curious as to why so few people do their own bagging; most customers stand passively by and wait for the employee to bag their groceries, sometimes a process which adds five minutes to the shopping experience.

Why should the customer participate in the delivery of the service? Obviously one reason is to improve the delivery of that service, either in time or in terms of preferences. But it is also possible that by increasing customer involvement, more customization of that service is possible, which should increase customer satisfaction. Gronroos (1988) insists that customers care not just about the outcome of the service but about the process itself–an assertion that I find problematical–and one that provides much of the basis for the "service quality" movement.

When I was in the trust business, we always joked about liking customer input into the investment selection process, even for accounts for which the bank had sole discretion, because "if the stocks go down, we can blame the customer." There is more than a grain of truth in the proposition that a customer who participates in the delivery of the service will feel more ownership in that service than someone who does not. If my eggs are crushed because I put them at the bottom of the bag, I have no complaint with the store; if the bagger does something like that, then the store should give me another dozen eggs. But for most customers, this almost-negative incentive is probably not enough to get them to participate more in the delivery process; something more is needed.

One potential incentive is, of course, a price discount or the chance for a greater selection of alternatives. An example of a discount which some banks have used in the past is to allow customers to pay their utility bills at the Automatic Teller Machines for free, but charge a service fee if they pay at the teller window. This has rarely seemed successful, perhaps because most people who pay their utility bills at a bank, rather than direct (or more recently by direct debit by the utility company) are not those who are major ATM users. However, this is an approach that needs to be monitored and probably fostered. Further, the influence of customers' word-of-mouth and referrals upon the service must be considered. Increasing customer participation may, in some cases, increase referrals and favorable word-of-mouth (File, Judd, and Prince, 1992).

I would like to return to the automation-of-services theme, first mentioned in Chapter 2. This time, though, I would like to present an idea that might make the automation efforts work better. Automation that allows (or forces) the customer to do some of the work should make automation efforts more successful, based on the thoughts given above on the subject of customer input. One service with which I am intimately familiar–although I have not previously dealt with it extensively as an automation issue–is InfoVision (Cahill, 1990). InfoVision is an integrated system consisting of a personal computer, super-high-resolution monitor, and a printer. The system has the capability of dealing with a large data base of real estate classified listings including both the text for advertising them as well as photographs of the property. By the end of 1988, the program could write ads in real time and display several photographs of a single property in a planned sequence, allowing the viewer to take a "tour" through the house. The viewer controlled all this interactively through a touchscreen, which required no computer literacy on the viewer's part. InfoVision started in 1985 as the concept of AJH, husband of one of the DECOY, Inc. managers. He saw that there could be a better way of delivering the information to the consumer–interactive, in color, and delivered to the mall where the consumer was spending large amounts of time. He foresaw one of these machines in every mall in the country, linked together electronically, delivering information to consumers for a fee.

Although InfoVision never attained commercial success, it was at one point on the cutting edge of interactive technology and delivery of information. As many steps in the delivery of information about houses for sale that could be automated had been. But user input was relegated to the selection of search parameters on the part of a potential buyer. There was no possibility for any input on the part of the seller of the house, who would, after all, be the person paying for the service. The picture for display was taken by a professional photographer, the advertising copy was written by a computer program based upon a form filled out by the real estate agent. Sellers had no input into the process and seemed somewhat reluctant to see their houses on the system. Realtors did not want to spend their advertising budgets there, either.

Hypothesize, rather, a system where a house seller comes to the InfoVision kiosk with a picture that the seller has taken and inputs herself. Advertising copy will be written by the same computer program, but the seller will fill out the form. (I can testify to the power of filling out this form for my own house; I first became intrigued by *CompuAd* by filling out the form on my own house, one whose every defect I know, and watching the system create an ad that made me want to buy the house all over again.) Sellers would then, I feel, be much more eager to see their houses on the system and would pressure their agents to advertise there. There is great power in customer input; but the computer system would automate all of the potential problem areas, such as improper language in the advertisement that might run afoul of various levels of regulatory enforcement. The system could also automate positively, such as prioritizing the features of the house to make it more attractive to potential buyers. There is great potency in a computerized, automated system that is properly designed.

What does that leave us for operations that cannot be, or at least are not yet, automated? Simply put, service business the old way? That is a prescription for failure. Old wine in new bottles: the old way (manually) with the new bottle of a well-designed internal marketing program, infused with new organization of the work to allow customer input in areas where the customer can do a better job than the firm can possibly do. I believe that this is a prescription for service firm success in the years ahead. But there is more needed than just new bottles for the old wine.

Wine has a way of going bad if left in the bottle too long, and putting it in new bottles may not stop the process (in fact, may actually accelerate the process it is designed to stop)–and sometimes the power of the wine destroys the new bottles.

LEARNING ORGANIZATIONS

There is a relatively new concept in the world of organizational science called the "Learning Organization." Although there is not a good parsimonious, general definition of learning organization, Watkins and Marsick (1993:xii) give five statements about what a learning organization is and is not:

1. It is not just a collection of individuals who are learning.
2. It demonstrates organizational capacity for change.
3. It accelerates individual learning capacity but also redefines organizational structure, culture, job design, and assumptions about the way things are.
4. It involves widespread participation of employees–and often customers–in decision making and information sharing.
5. It promotes systematic thinking and building of organizational memory.

Notice how "fuzzy" this list is; many results of organizational learning are not quantifiable. However, this does not mean that they are unknowable. Organizational learning, unlike quality management, is not engineer driven; systems thinking may be a scientific discipline, but it does not insist that everything worth knowing be quantified or even quantifiable. And organizational learning has probably become the critical competency of the 1990s (Dixon, 1992).

I would add to this list that the learning organization *understands* its culture and the impact that being a learning organization has upon the firm's culture and the reciprocal impact that the culture has upon the firm's ability to learn. Culture, as socially constructed realities, is important to the organization; using the plural of reality implies that culture is an evolving process based on a changing definition of reality (Thompson and Luthans, 1990). Thompson and Luthans (pp. 328-337) further state several properties that emerge when relating behavioral and learning principles to organizational culture:

1. Culture is a generic term.
2. Culture is learned.
3. Culture is transmitted through a pattern of behavioral interactions.
4. In an organizational setting, there are multiple reinforcements and reinforcing agents.
5. Each individual carries predispositions that shape his or her interpretation of the organizational culture.
6. A symbiotic relationship exists between the reinforcing agent and target.
7. Changing an established culture is difficult.

Senge (1990) lists several "learning disabilities" that are ingrained in all organizations; these learning disabilities will get in the way of any attempt to change an existing organization into a learning organization:

1. "I am my position"–the manager or employee who places loyalty to the job before loyalty to the firm, what Tobin (1993) calls "functional myopia."
2. "The enemy is out there"–the true enemy is almost invariably "in here."
3. The illusion of taking charge–proactivity is "reactiveness in disguise."
4. The fixation on events rather than processes.
5. The delusion of learning from experience–but the fact remains that we rarely directly suffer the consequences of

many of our decisions because of the temporal separation of decision and consequence.

6. The myth of the management "team."

Senge is one of Jay Forrester's systems gurus at the Massachusetts Institute of Technology; as such, he sees most of the solution to the above learning disabilities in the adoption of systems thinking by organizations and their participants. This viewpoint suffuses his book *The Fifth Discipline* (systems thinking) and his view of organizational learning accordingly suffers from too narrow a focus while seeming to be very broad in scope. There is more to organizational learning than getting everyone to understand systems and their architectures. His statement of the essence of the discipline of systems thinking (Senge, 1990:73) is a case in point; the essence lies in a shift of mind to seeing interrelationships rather than linear cause-and-effect chains and seeing processes rather than static pictures. This is a cogent definition of the essence of systems thinking, and a holistic viewpoint (and processual viewpoint as well) always comes in handy; however, neither is sufficient (nor are both) and the tools of systems thinking clutter the book unnecessarily. Nevertheless, Senge's book is crucial to any understanding of learning organizations, if for no other reason than its focus upon the role of structure on behavior, a role that is often overlooked or ignored in modern studies in many fields and the fact that every subsequent book on the subject cites it. In a later book (Senge et al., 1994:18), Senge has changed the definition of the essence of the learning organization to the development—not just of new capacities but of fundamental shifts of individual and collective minds; I believe that this change obviates some of my concern about relying totally on systems thinking.

We are now coming to understand that there are four groups of concepts that need attending to in order to build an organizational foundation for the learning organization: Philosophy (in which vision, values, and purpose are important), Attitudes and Beliefs (in which there is genuine caring, a communality of purpose, and the willingness to admit lack of knowledge), Skills and Capabilities (in which systems thinking is developed, along with a shared commitment), and Tools (in which the systems devices Senge develops in [1990] and [1994] are used throughout the organization). Developing this foundation and the new organizational skills and capabilities which need to flow from them may be the "highest-leverage area for creating lasting change" (Senge, 1993:21).

Senge (1990) further focuses tightly on the necessity of having a shared vision throughout the organization. In fact he flatly states (p. 209) that one "cannot have a learning organization without shared vision. Without a pull toward some goal which people truly want to achieve, the forces in support of the status quo can be overwhelming." Further, shared vision provides the focus and energy for learning. "It's not what the vision is, it's what the vision does" that is important (Senge, 1990:154)–an example of his focus on the process rather than the product. The vision pulls the entire organization together, much as Jay's restatement of St. Augustine's "Please God and do as you like." Bennett and O'Brien (1994) studied 25 successful learning organizations; they found that the first principle is the need for a vision on which organizational members can base their future learning requirements.

In a chapter on localness with a subhead entitled "How Do You Achieve Control Without Controlling?" Senge focuses on the systems aspects of the question, completely missing the import of the statement by St. Augustine. One achieves control without controlling by possessing the minds of those who are "out there on the front lines"–exactly as Jay describes the process. *This* is shared vision; what Senge often seems to claim as shared vision appears to me to be more along the lines of an individual vision implanted by a process that he fails to describe. St. Augustine's point is that the vision, "loving God," comes from within only after one truly understands "God." It is the ability to handle people by inculcating the organization's beliefs and values–its shared vision–into each and every employee. And the only way to do this is to have beliefs and values that all employees can share, can want, and can live with happily. Not imposed from above by "leaders" or "managers"–the "managerial elite"–but genuinely, positively shared. Generated by all, from janitor to chairman. Senge does not deal with the differences between small and large firms, one-site versus geographically dispersed organizations, entrepreneurially owned versus publicly held. And there is no real reason for him to have. Learning organizations can be any of the above; what seems to me to be the most important criterion of being a learning organization is that it have a shared vision.

A concrete application of the concept of a learning organization lies in the planning process. Stacey's (1992) is one of a plethora of recent books and articles claiming that for various reasons strategic planning does not work–or, at the very least, the old ways of planning no longer work. Stacey's complaint is that the currently hot concept of chaos (or what he calls "bounded instability") makes it impossible to know the future and thus plan for it. Cahill (1989), Daft and Lengel (1993), and O'Gorman (1993) have also all addressed chaos and strategic planning, all with different conclusions from those that Stacey draws.

Stacey feels that vision will not help, that there is no proven connection between planning and results–betraying his focus on planning as a product ("the plan") rather than on planning as a process. He then presents the idea of a "self-organizing" coalition to form within the larger organization to promote "self-learning" and interface with the chaotic environment. Stacey is offended by planning from the top down (as I am, and I would guess most modern writers are), by "charismatic" leaders formulating a vision of what the organization should become and trying to push the organization along a path that would get it there.

> As soon as we recognize that the dynamic of a successful company is chaotic and the long-term future is unknowable, it becomes clear that long-term plans, mission statements, and visions are also bypass games. These abstract statements without operational content, are produced simply to convey an impression of rational decision making and to keep people quiet or secure. (Stacey, 1992:116)

To say that the future is unknowable is frivolous; of course it is unknowable, unless one is an omniscient god. What Stacey seems to miss, or ignore, about the process of visions, and corporate missions, and all the other panoply of strategic planning as it has been practiced, is that it all is directed at a *goal*. Of course one cannot *know* what the results of these plans will be, but one can try to focus the organization in the direction it should be traveling.

And herein lies a crucial part of Senge's argument and of his focus on process rather than product. Planning is a process; the plan is a product. *Planning* is important–planning must be a learning exercise, valuable in and of itself. The plan then becomes secondary, a statement of the result of what the planners have learned about themselves and the organization. Who is on the planning team thus becomes less important than the fact that there is a team planning and presenting the thoughts and assumptions behind the planning to the organization as a whole. This is planning that does not produce a multi-volume plan to bind in a black notebook at the end of the year that will be allowed to gather dust–or, worse, be used to control individuals in the organization in the coming year–but rather a living document that can breathe life into the organization's future efforts.

Why all this emphasis on "learning organizations" in a book on internal marketing? Simply put, I believe that the metamorphosis of an organization into a learning organization is a necessary step in the correct performance of internal marketing. Unlike a "pure" or "classical" learning organization, which Senge and others would claim learns for the sheer sake of learning—that this is the culmination of all the "empowerment" and "human factors design" or organizations, the jump from "Theory X to Theory Y to Learning Organizations," that we should go toward learning organizations because it is the "right" (ethical) thing to do, I preach the learning organization concept purely to drive organizations toward internal marketing. Although I agree that most employees in traditional organizations are systematically mistreated in many ways, I am more interested here in the application of the concept as a tool to get the organization to provide its services to its customers better, with more competence and understanding of who the customers are and what they want. *That* is why I believe in learning organizations. Without this core of learning—and the ability to pass that learning on from generation to generation (and in firms with annual employee and supervisor turnover rates of 25 percent or more being considered "normal," not to mention the rise of "leased" and temporary employees as long-term staffing solutions, an employee generation is two or three years at best)—the organization cannot provide its services to its customers with more competence and understanding. Period.

And all of this implies or requires an organizational memory and the ability of that memory to pass on what it remembers. Organizational memory's core is information about decisions made and problems solved. Walsh and Ungson (1991) make clear that memory is not centrally stored, but distributed across the organization—the same decentralization/distribution pattern that Jay so clearly calls for in his descriptions of the decentralized organization. There are, of course, pluses and minuses to organizational memory. At its best, organizational memory allows the organization to call up past events, remember what was done, what worked and what did not, and not have to "reinvent the wheel." At its worst, organizational memory becomes drill, rote learning, constraining the organization to do what it did in the past, regardless of changing conditions.

Most of us know of examples of organizational memory at its best, conditioning the organization to remember what worked in the past and learn from that experience. I have played on baseball teams that reached levels far above the summation of the abilities of the individual members because the team was able to learn. This is what happens when a new (possibly great) second baseman is brought along to be paired up with a great shortstop. For a time, their ability as a team, particularly their ability to turn double plays, is *less* than the sum of their great individual abilities; eventually they may become a great keystone combination, but only when they play as a team and learn as a team. This is what Dodger manager Tommy Lasorda means about "Dodger Blue"; there is a team *persona,* a team identity that infuses the whole team and not just each member of that team as an individual.

This concept of "Dodger Blue" or the United Parcel Service statement that an employee "Bleeds Brown Blood" can help an organization withstand traumatic environmental shocks. When Central National Bank went through its disastrous period in the early 1980s that ultimately led to its demise, employees–particularly senior employees–left in droves, finding new jobs in the banking industry or taking early retirement. In a one-year period, 20 vice presidents or senior vice presidents left the trust department–out of approximately 60 officers of all grades. In circumstances like this, continuity of effort becomes difficult; at Central it proved impossible, for there was no hard core of learning or "culture" that could withstand the trauma. And perhaps this is what many authors truly mean by "strong" culture–a term that has baffled many academic writers on culture; a "strong" culture is merely one which can withstand such shocks, that can help its organization learn as an organization.

A personal example of organizational learning at its worst, fossilizing into rote performance of duties not understood (or, perhaps, not understandable) happened to me at Medusa Cement, my first post-MBA employer. After I had been assistant credit manager for about six months, my boss asked me to prepare our department's month-end "Blue Book" page. The "Blue Book" consisted of one-page summaries of financial information, department by department, in a format that the then-Chairman of Medusa Corporation had dictated well over a decade earlier. I spent an entire day with the previous month's report, prepared by our accounts receivable clerk, and the current trial balance data, trying to deal with the report. I gave the report to the clerk to check before sending it upstairs–only to be told that every item on it was wrong. Every label on our report was misleading, every number came from somewhere other than where it "should have" based upon its name, etc. When I protested to my boss that the Blue Book was a travesty, that it did not accurately report any figure except possibly our Day's Sales Outstanding (and I felt that the way it calculated that figure was misleading at best–it reported a higher number than the standard calculation did), I was told that I was absolutely right, "But that is the way the Chairman is used to seeing the numbers and that is the way he wants them." I never prepared the Blue Book again in over two years of further employment at Medusa. Everyone knew the numbers were meaningless, but organizational learning had fossilized what was being done. I subsequently learned that when the Chairman had designed the Blue Book, Medusa kept its books differently and the report made sense at the time, but that when the accounting system changed, no one thought to go through the reports to see if anything would need to be altered. The result was, of course, that Chairman got a meaningless report that he thought he understood, but the basis for the numbers that he thought he understood was not what he thought was their basis.

"Learning in organizations means the continuous testing of experience, and the transformation of that experience into knowledge–accessible to the whole organization, and relevant to its core purpose" (Senge et al., 1994:49). Notice the words "continuous testing of experience"; to a great extent, this is the crux of the whole argument. Not only must experience be continuously tested (for a purpose, not just to test), but the relevant knowledge that is produced must be shared with everyone in the organization. Thus I continually emphasize training employees beyond competence in their professional field, training them on what it means to be an employee of the organization.

As an example of the continuous testing and sharing of the results, Kline and Saunders (1993:72) state that the usual practice of paying attention to complaining customers is "nonthinking"–ignoring why the current practice of paying attention to these customers developed in the first place. This statement runs counter, of course, to the consumer satisfaction/dissatisfaction literature (both academic and practitioner) which encourages organizations to seek out the complainers and get them to complain in detail. Of course, Kline and Saunders have a point; the usual Pareto utility (often known as the "80/20 Rule") runs here, too–at least 80 percent of the complaints will be generated by 20 percent of the customers (and Murphy's Law assures us that the complaining 20 percent probably buy very little from us). Nevertheless, the prime reason for seeking to pull out complaints is twofold: First, people who are satisfied with our product or service will be able to tell us very little how we need to improve; second, people with complaints can often be encouraged to talk, and satisfied customers, for all practical purposes, do not exist in the communications stream. Organizational experience with complaining customers can be turned into information which can be shared throughout the organization and is thus vital if the organization is to be a learning organization.

Appendix 1

Addresses of Institutions Mentioned

Association for Psychological Type
9140 Ward Parkway
Kansas City, MO 64114
(816) 444-3500

Consulting Psychologists Press, Inc.
3803 E. Bayshore Rd.
Palo Alto, CA 94303
(415) 969-8901

SRI International
333 Ravenswood Ave.
Menlo Park, CA 94025
(419) 859-4324

Appendix 2

Marketing Typologies

Segmentation schemes or typologies abound in the academic marketing literature. Almost every issue of the *Journal of Marketing* or *Journal of Marketing Research* presents a new typological approach to some aspect of marketing. Why? One reason is that the creation of typologies is academically respectable, and its respectability will probably increase after Doty and Glick's (1994) claim that typologies are, in fact, theories–if properly constructed.

Formal segmentation schemes have, however, not been as much in evidence in the practitioner's world. There seem to be two reasons for this. First, in cases where there is a formal scheme being used by a firm, it is usually proprietary and not mentioned outside of the firm or its advertising agency. Second, the overabundance of schemes available is confusing and counterproductive for practitioners, most of whom have neither the time, nor in many cases, the mathematical skills necessary to determine which of the dozens of possible typologies available would do the best job for the firm with the least cost and effort. Do we really need another segmentation scheme? Are there not enough around which deal with demographics, or geography, or other variables? Do we need another?

I would argue that we probably do not. VALS works. As pointed out in Chapter 3, it even works in an organizational setting as a communication tool. Why does it work? VALS attempted to deal with consumers' values; the List of Values segmentation method also attempts to deal with them. They are, however, only pragmatic applications of the original Rokeach Value Survey, done by a famous social psychologist from Michigan State University 40 years ago. Rokeach devised a list of 36 values: 18 were what he called "Terminal Values" and 18 were what he called "Instrumental Values"–that is, values that get one to where one wants to be (the Terminal Values). (For an in-depth discussion of the Rokeach Value Survey see Rokeach [1968, 1979]; the once universal acceptance of Rokeach has begun to erode–see Zenzen and Hammer [1978] and Braithwaite and Law [1985].) The purpose of Rokeach's Survey is to group people into various cohorts of similar outlooks in an attempt to communicate with them about "Great Issues." Values marketing segmentation seeks to group people into cohorts, not to communicate about Great Issues, but not to sell them more toilet paper, either. Values segmentation at its root seeks to group people in order to understand them better and to communicate with them non-manipulatively.

When Arnold Mitchell and his team at SRI created VALS–combining Rokeach's work with values and Maslow's psychological work with individuals' hierarchies of needs–they did so because they felt that values tell a lot about a person and answer practical questions of interest to social scientists (Mitchell, 1983:vii). Only later was VALS developed into a marketing typology. Nevertheless, it came along at a time when others were doing values research with a marketing bent; in fact Vinson, Scott, and Lamont (1977) claim that values are both theoretically important in studying consumer behavior and of practical relevance to marketing managers. Pitts and Woodside (1984) published a book aimed directly at values and consumer psychology; many of the articles in the book were reports by managers of their experiences in using values as a segmentation tool.

This is one of the sources of VALS' strength. Practicing managers can readily understand the scheme and its implications after only a bit of reading and a short seminar, as described in Chapter 3. A graphic of the VALS typology may be seen in *The Nine American Lifestyles: Who We Are and Where We're Going* (Mitchell, 1983). VALS works nationwide, with some regional variation in the composition of the various types (Ashyk, 1988). Of course, other psychographic schemes may also be generalizable; Lesser and Hughes (1986) studied schemes developed for 17 different cities and discovered that such schemes seem to be generalizable. Kahle (1986) applies his List of Values to the country as a whole. Another source of VALS' strength has always been the ongoing research effort made by SRI to dig deeper into its service and extend the segmentation to other areas. Over the years, SRI published reports on VALS and the experience industry (Ogilvy, 1985), media usage by VALS types (Kimball, 1982), VALS types and innovation (Walling, 1984), among many others. This research enabled VALS users to approach similar problems with a great leg up in understanding.

Nevertheless, VALS came under criticism, primarily from the academic community. In 1983, Lynn Kahle threw down the gauntlet, basically claiming that since VALS was proprietary and SRI had never released any of its data and results through peer-reviewed journals, the whole scheme was suspect. He developed a new instrument for values segmentation, called the List of Values and released it with a plea for continued research on both LOV and VALS (Kahle, Beatty, and Homer, 1986). And the debate was engaged. In a special issue of *Psychology and Marketing* which he edited (Kahle, 1985), Kahle presented some of the further research he had called for. The SRI people responded, somewhat hobbled by the fact that VALS *is* proprietary and they could not disclose to the academics what the academics truly wanted to see (Novak and MacEvoy, 1990).

Much of the usefulness in VALS seems to me to have gone out of the service when SRI, for reasons that must have made sense to them, created VALS 2 in the late 1980s (Riche, 1989). It seemed to me–and to others (Winters, 1989)–that this was a case of the maxim "if it ain't broke, don't fix it" being ignored. The VALS 2 scheme is less values-driven and–according to the people at SRI–both more universal and more enduring. Time will tell.

Although there are few guidelines to creating values segmentation schemes, and none that I know of for their use in internal marketing programs, I believe that this may be an area with potential in the future. Segmentation schemes have a few basic requirements (Cravens and Woodruff, 1986:215-216):

1. Are there differences in responsiveness between segments?
2. Can the people in each segment be identified?

3. Is it feasible to aim different messages to different segments?
4. Is segmentation worth doing in this case?
5. Will the segments remain stable over time?

These questions were mostly answered in the affirmative for VALS; see Chapter 3 for that discussion.

Kahle calls the feasibility of aiming different messages at different segments and the worth of doing segmentation with VALS into question by positing that a long, involved process is necessary to create a "VALS-speak" advertisement. It was not my experience that this six-step process (Kahle 1985:234) has any validity. He states that one must (1) create a consumer survey, (2) VALS-classify the respondents, (3) have an account executive at the advertising agency interpret the classification results, (4) weigh the client's desires as related to the foregoing interpretation, (5) have a creative person from the agency render "these opinions" in an advertisement, which is that (6) directed back at the consumer. Kahle next states that "we have traveled a long distance from the potential consumer in the survey" at Step 1 by the end of this process (Kahle 1985:234). I would have to agree with this last statement if the technique outlined was what actually happens. What happens at most is that one creates a research instrument *with the VALS typing instrument contained therein*. There is no need for Step 2, then–since it is done in one step–nor are Steps 3 and 4 necessary as, in a very short period of time, everyone "speaks VALS" fluently. What typically happens is that one VALS-types one's market once, or at most occasionally, then deals with the "reality" that the typology shows to be present. This reduces Kahle's six steps to two: making sure that the "creative" at the agency understands VALS, and then reviewing the agency's work for VALS' correctness before exposing it to the target market segments. For internal marketing, the process would be even more streamlined once the organization had been VALS-typed.

List of Values has not truly faced some of these questions, most notably the stability of the LOV segments over time. However, even the validity of the LOV has been called into question; Herche (1994) reports that his "Multi-item List of Values" (MILOV) explains almost twice as many variations in behavior as the original LOV.

Nevertheless, some segmentation of internal sections seems to be necessary before an internal marketing program can be properly designed and implemented. If we are getting away from mass marketing in our external markets, it makes little or no sense to assume that our internal marketing efforts are going to be well designed if they approach their market–our employees–as though they were a homogeneous mass.

References

Abuse on Wall Street: Conflicts of Interest in the Securities Markets. A Twentieth Century Fund Staff. (1980). Westport, CT: Quorum Books.

Aristotle (1981). *Aristotle's Poetics: A Translation and Commentary for Students of Literature.* Translated by Leon Golden. Tallahassee: Florida State University Press.

Ashyk, Lori (1988). "WJW's Market Survey Finds Clevelanders Ache to Achieve," *Crain's Cleveland Business,* (August 22), p. 13.

Atlas, James (1984). "Beyond Demographics," *The Atlantic Monthly,* October, pp. 49-58.

Axson, David A. J. (1992). "A Return to Managing Customer Relationships," *The International Journal of Bank Marketing,* Vol. 10, #1, pp. 30-35.

Bak, Constance A., Leslie H. Vogt, William R. George, and I. Richard Greentree (1994). "Management By Team: An Innovative Tool for Running a Service Organization Through Internal Marketing," *Journal of Services Marketing,* Vol, 8, #1, pp. 37-47.

Balombin, Clare (1987). "President's Club: Successful Internal Marketing at BancOhio," in John A. Czepiel, Carole A. Congram, and James Shanahan (eds.), *The Services Challenge: Integrating for Competitive Advantage.* Proceedings of the 5th Annual Services Marketing Conference. Chicago: American Marketing Association, pp. 21-22.

Beck, David (1992). "Implementing a Gainsharing Plan: What Companies Need to Know," *Compensation & Benefits Review,* January-February, pp. 21-33.

Bennett, Joan Kremer and Michael J. O'Brien (1994). "The 12 Building Blocks of the Learning Organization," *Training,* Vol. 31 (June), pp. 41-48.

Berry, Dick (1988). "The Marketing Concept Revisited: It's Setting Goals, Not Making a Mad Dash for Profits," *Marketing News,* July 18, pp. 26, 28.

Berry, Leonard L. and A. Parasuraman (1991). *Marketing Services: Competing Through Quality.* New York: The Free Press.

Berton, Lee (1989). "Innovating Means Taking Time From Same Old Grind," *The Wall Street Journal,* August 31, p. B2.

Bitran, Gabrial R. and Johannes Hoech (1990). "The Humanization of Service: Respect at the Moment of Truth," *Sloan Management Review,* Winter, pp. 89-96.

Braithwaite, V. A. and H. G. Law (1985). "Structure of Human Values: Testing the Adequacy of the Rokeach Value Survey," *Journal of Personality and Social Psychology,* Vol. 49, #1, pp. 250-263.

Brock, Susan A. and Lawrence Demarest (1989). "Flexible Selling: Using Type in the Sales Process," in Naomi L. Quenk (ed.), *Frontiers of Psychological Type: Proceedings of APT-VIII.* Gainesville, FL: Association for Psychological Type, pp. 112-115.

Burke, Raymond R., Arvind Rangaswamy, Jerry Wind, and Jehoshua Eliashberg (1988). "ADCAD: A Knowledge-Based System for Advertising Design." Working Paper #88-027. Philadelphia: Wharton School of the University of Pennsylvania.

Burns, Tom and G. M. Stalker (1961). *The Management of Innovation*. London: Tavistock Institute.

Cahill, Dennis J. (1989). "*De Revolutionibus Scientii*: Or, Is a Paradigm Really Worth Less Than a Quarter." Address given to the Rowfant Society, March 23.

_______ (1990). "Industrializing Services: An Example of What Not to Do," in *Stayin' Alive Through '95: How to Thrive and Not Just Survive,* 9th Annual Services Marketing Conference. Chicago: American Marketing Association, pp. 52-63.

_______ (1992a). "I Want a Choice, Not the 'Standard' Excuse," *Marketing News,* January 6, pp. 4, 32.

_______ (1992b). "It's Time for Santa, the Marketing Genius," *Marketing News,* December 7, p. 4.

_______ (1992c). "The Winter Olympics as a Services Marketing Paradigm," *Services Marketing Today,* May/June, p. 4.

_______ (1993). "Innovation and the Professional Service Organization," *Journal of Professional Services Marketing,* Vol. 10, #1, pp. 147-159.

_______ (1995). *Squeezing a New Service into a Crowded Marketplace*. Binghamton, NY: The Haworth Press.

_______ (1996). "What's Wrong With Service Providers?: A Customer-Service Perspective," *The Journal of Customer Service in Marketing & Management*, Vol. 2, #3.

_______ and Robert M. Warshawsky (1993). "The Marketing Concept: A Forgotten Aid for Marketing High-Technology Products," *Journal of Consumer Marketing*, Vol. 10, #1, pp. 12-22.

_______ (1995). "Beyond Competence: Unconditional Guarantees as a Customer Service Tool," *Journal of Customer Service in Marketing & Management,* Vol. 1, #2, Spring/Summer, 1995.

Cahill, Dennis J., Robert M. Warshawsky and Sharon V. Thach (1994). "From Experience: The Marketing Concept and New High-Tech Products: Is There a Fit?" *The Journal of Product Innovation Management,* Vol. 11, #4, September.

Close to the Customer: An American Management Association Research Report on Consumer Affairs (1987). Chicago: AMACOM.

Compton, Fran (1987). "Internal Marketing of Marketing," in John A. Czepiel, Carole A. Congram, and James Shanahan (eds.), *The Services Challenge: Integrating for Competitive Advantage.* Proceedings of the 5th Annual Services Marketing Conference. Chicago: American Marketing Association, pp. 17-20.

Compton, Fran, William R. George, Christian Gronroos, and Matti Karvinen (1987). "Internal Marketing," in John A. Czepiel, Carole A. Congram, and James Shanahan (eds.), *The Services Challenge: Integrating for Competitive Advantage.* Proceedings of the 5th Annual Services Marketing Conference. Chicago: American Marketing Association, pp. 7-12.

Cravens, David W. and Robert B. Woodruff (1986). *Marketing.* Reading, MA: Addison-Wesley.

Crawford, John C. (1983). "The Marketing Concept–A Utopian Dream?" in John C. Rogers, III (ed.), *Developments in Marketing Science, VI*. Logan, UT: Academy of Marketing Science, pp. 450-452.

Daft, Richard L. and Robert H. Lengel (1993). "The Challenge of Chaos: An Idea Borrowed from the World of Science Has Wide-reaching Implications for Management," *Beta Gamma Sigma News,* Fall, pp. 1, 5-6. Originally in *Owen Manager,* Spring, 1993.

Dauw, Dean C. (1969). "Bridging the Creativity-Innovation Gap," *The Journal of Creative Behavior,* Spring, pp. 84-89.

Davidow, William H. (1986). *Marketing High Technology: An Insider's View.* NY: The Free Press.

Davidow, William H. and Bro Uttal (1989). "Service Companies: Focus or Falter," *Harvard Business Review,* July-August, pp. 75-85.

Demby, Emanuel H. (1989). "Psychographics Revisited: The Birth of a Technique," *Marketing News,* January 2, p. 21.

Deshpande, Rohit and Frederick C. Webster, Jr. (1989). "Organizational Culture and Marketing: Defining the Research Agenda," *Journal of Marketing,* January, pp. 3-15.

DiTomaso, Nancy (1987). "Symbolic Media and Social Solidarity: The Foundations of Corporate Culture," in *Research in the Sociology of Organizations, V.* Greenwich, CT: JAI Press, Inc., pp. 105-134.

Dixon, Nancy M. (1992). "Organizational Learning: A Review of the Literature with Implications for HRD Professionals," *Human Resource Development Quarterly,* Vol. 3, #1 (Spring), pp. 29-49.

Doherty, Elizabeth M., Walter R. Nord, and Jerry L. McAdams (1989). "Gainsharing and Organization Development: A Productive Synergy," *The Journal of Applied Behavioral Science,* Fall, pp. 209-229.

Doty, D. Harold and William H. Glick (1994). "Typologies As a Unique Form of Theory Building: Toward Improved Understanding and Modeling," *The Academy of Management Review,* Vol. 19, #2, pp. 230-251.

Edwards, Mark R. and J. Ruth Sproull (1984). "Creativity" Productivity Gold Mine?" *The Journal of Creative Behavior,* Summer, pp. 175-184.

Evans, Joel R. and Barry Berman (1987). *Marketing,* 3rd. ed., New York: Macmillan.

File, Karen Maru, Ben B. Judd, and Russ Alan Prince (1992). "Interactive Marketing: The Influence of Participation on Positive Word-of-Mouth and Referrals," *Journal of Services Marketing,* Vol. 6, #4 (Fall), pp. 5-14.

Fox, Isaac and Alfred Marcus (1992). "The Causes and Consequences of Leveraged Management Buyouts," *Academy of Management Review,* January, pp. 62-85.

Foxall, Gordon R. and Ronald E. Goldsmith (1994). *Consumer Psychology for Marketing.* London: Routledgc.

George, William R. (1990). "Internal Marketing and Organizational Behavior: A Partnership in Developing Customer-Conscious Employees at Every Level," *Journal of Business Research,* Vol. 20, pp. 63-70.

Goldberg, Andy (1991). *Improv Comedy.* Hollywood, CA: Samuel French.

Goodman, Paul S. and James W. Dean, Jr. (1990). "Making Productivity Programs Last," in Brian Graham-Moore and Timothy L. Ross (eds.), *Gainsharing: Plans for Improving Performance.* Washington: Bureau of National Affairs, pp. 116-135.

Graham-Moore, Brian (1990a). "Formulas for Developing a Reward Structure to Further Organizational Goals," in Brian Graham-Moore and Timothy L. Ross (eds.) *Gainsharing: Plans for Improving Performance.* Washington: Bureau of National Affairs, pp. 48-80.

______ (1990b). "Review of the Literature," in Brian Graham-Moore and Timothy L. Ross (eds.), *Gainsharing: Plans for Improving Performance.* Washington: Bureau of National Affairs, pp. 19-47.

Gronroos, Christian (1981a). "Internal Marketing–An Integral Part of Marketing Theory," in American Marketing Association Services Marketing Conference *Proceedings,* pp. 236-238.

_______ (1981b). "Internal Marketing–Theory and Practice," in *American Marketing Association Services Marketing Conference Proceedings,* pp. 41-47.

_______ (1988). "A Service Quality Model and Its Marketing Implications," *European Journal of Marketing,* Vol. 18, #4, pp. 36-44.

_______ (1994). "From Marketing Mix to Relationship Marketing: Towards a Paradigm Shift in Marketing," *Management Decision,* Vol. 32, #2, pp. 4-20.

Grove, Stephen J. and Raymond P. Fisk (1989). "Impression Management in Services Marketing: A Dramaturgical Perspective," in Robert A. Giacalone and Paul Rosenfeld (eds.) *Impression Management in the Organization*. Hillsdale, NJ: Lawrence Erlbaum Associates, pp. 427-438.

_______ (1992). "The Service Experience as Theater." *Advances in Consumer Research,* XIX. Provo, UT: Association of Consumer Research, pp. 455-461.

Guaspari, John (1988). *The Customer Connection: Quality for the Rest of Us*. Chicago: AMACOM.

Gummesson, Evert (1987). "Using Internal Marketing to Develop a New Culture–The Case of Ericsson Quality," in John A. Czepiel, Carole A. Congram, and James Shanahan (eds.), *The Services Challenge: Integrating for Competitive Advantage.* Proceedings of the 5th Annual Services Marketing Conference. Chicago: American Marketing Association, pp. 13-15.

Gupta, Ashok K. and Everett M. Rogers (1991). "Internal Marketing: Integrating R & D and Marketing Within the Organization," *The Journal of Services Marketing,* Vol. 5, #2, (Spring), pp. 55-68.

Haberman, Ian S. (1979). *The Van Sweringens of Cleveland: The Biography of an Empire.* Cleveland, OH: The Western Reserve Historical Society.

Habermas, Jürgen (1984). *The Theory of Communicative Action: Reason and the Rationalization of Society, I,* translated by Thomas McCarthy. Boston: Beacon Press.

Hackett, Gregory P. (1990). "Investment in Technology–The Service Sector Sinkhole," *Sloan Management Review,* Winter, pp. 97-103.

Hampton, Gerald M. and Emmett Lane (1982). "Newspapers and the Marketing Concept: An Exploratory Study of the Attitudes of Newsroom and Management Personnel," in Vinay Kothari (ed.) *Developments in Marketing Science,* V. Nagodoches, TX: Academy of Marketing Science, pp. 450-455.

Hart, Christopher W. L. (1988). "The Power of Unconditional Service Guarantees," *Harvard Business Review,* July-August, pp. 54-62.

Hawkins, Del I., Roger J. Best, and Kenneth A. Coney (1986). *Consumer Behavior: Implications for Marketing Strategy,* 3rd ed. Plano, TX: Business Publications.

Henderson, Bruce (1988). "Letter," *Harvard Business Review,* September-October, p. 172.

Herche, Joel (1994). "Measuring Social Values: A Multi-item Adaptation to the List of Values (MILOV)." Cambridge, MA: Marketing Science Institute, Technical Working Paper, pp. 94-101.

Hertzberg, Frederick (1973). "One More Time: How Do You Motivate Employees," *Harvard Business Review,* Vol. 51, # 3 (May-June), pp. 162-180.

Heskett, James L., W. Earl Sasser, Jr., and Christopher W. L. Hart (1990). *Service Breakthroughs: Changing the Rules of the Game.* New York: The Free Press.

Hirschman, Elizabeth C. (1983). "Aesthetics, Ideologies, and the Limits of the Marketing Concept," *Journal of Marketing,* Summer, pp. 45-55.

_______ (1980). "Commonality and Idiosyncrasy in Popular Culture: An Empirical Examination of the 'Layers of Meaning' Concept," in Elizabeth C. Hirschman and Morris B. Holbrook (eds.), *Symbolic Consumer Behavior.* Ann Arbor, MI: Association of Consumer Research.

Hoffman, K. Douglas and Thomas N. Ingram (1992). "Service Provider Job Satisfaction and Customer-Oriented Performance," *The Journal of Services Marketing,* Vol. 6, #2 (Spring), pp. 68-78.

Holliday, William G. (1993). "Right Attitudes and Sacred Habits." March 21. Sermon given at Plymouth Church of Shaker Heights, Ohio.

Ingersoll, Virginia Hill and Guy B. Adams (1992). *The Tacit Organization.* Greenwich, CT: JAI Press.

Jay, Anthony (1967). *Management and Machiavelli: An Inquiry into the Politics of Corporate Life.* NY: Holt, Rinehart and Winston.

Jelinek, Mariann and Claudia Bird Schoonhoven (1993). *The Innovation Marathon: Lessons from High Technology Firms.* San Francisco: Jossey-Bass.

Johnson, Eugene M., Eberhard E. Scheuing, and Kathleen A. Gaida (1986). *Profitable Services Marketing.* Homewood, IL: Dow-Jones Irwin.

Johnson, Eugene M. and Daniel T. Seymour (1985). "The Impact of Cross Selling on the Service Encounter in Retail Banking," in John A. Czepiel, Michael R. Solomon, and Carol Surprenant (eds.), *The Service Encounter: Managing Employee/Customer Interaction in Service Businesses.* Lexington, MA: Lexington Books, pp. 225-239.

Kahle, Lynn R. (ed.) (1983). *Social Values and Social Change: Adaptation to Life in America.* New York: Praeger.

_______ (1985). "Social Values in the Eighties: A Special Issue," *Psychology and Marketing,* pp. 231-237.

_______ (1986). "The Nine Nations of North America and the Value Basis of Geographic Segmentation," *Journal of Marketing,* Vol. 50 (April), pp. 37-47.

Kahle, Lynn R., Sharon E. Beatty, and Pamela Homer (1986). "Alternative Measurement Approaches to Consumer Values: The List of Values (LOV) and Values and Life Style (VALS)," *Journal of Consumer Research,* Vol. 13 (December), pp. 405-409.

Keirsey, David (1989). *Portraits of Temperament.* Del Mar, CA: Prometheus Nemesis Book.

Keirsey, David and Marilyn Bates (1984). *Please Understand Me: Character & Temperament Types.* Del Mar, CA: Prometheus Nemesis Book.

Kessing, Roger M. (1981). "Theories of Culture," in Ronald W. Casson (ed.) *Language, Culture and Cognition.* New York: Macmillan, pp. 41-66. Originally published in *Annual Review of Anthropology* (1974), pp. 73-97.

Kilmann, Ralph H., Mary J. Saxton, and Roy Serpa (1986). "Issues in Understanding and Changing Culture," *California Management Review,* pp. 87-109.

Kimball, Robert J. (1982). *Media Usage by the VALS Types.* Menlo Park, CA: SRI International.

Kline, Peter and Bernard Saunders (1993). *Ten Steps to a Learning Organization.* Arlington, VA: Great Occan Publishers.

Kohn, Alfie (1994). "Why Incentives Fail: An Interview," *CFO,* (September), pp. 15-16.

Lawrence, Gordon (1982). *People Types & Tiger Stripes: A Practical Guide to Learning Styles,* 2nd ed. Palo Alto, CA: Consulting Psychologists Press.

Lesser, Jack A. and Marie Adele Hughes (1986). "The Generalizability of Psychographic Market Segments Across Geographic Locations," *Journal of Marketing,* Vol. 50 (January), pp. 18-27.

Levitt, Theodore (1974). "The Industrialization of Service," *Harvard Business Review,* September-October, pp. 63-74.

Levy, Diane and Carol Surprenant (1982). "A Comparison of Responses to Dissatisfaction with Products and Services," in H. Keith Hunt and Ralph L. Day (eds.), *Conceptual and Empirical Contributions to Consumer Satisfaction and Complaining Behavior.* Bloomington, IN: Indiana University Press, pp. 43-49.

Martin, Charles L. (1994). "Editorial: Are Service Consumers Intangible Too?" *Journal of Services Marketing,* Vol. 8, #1, p. 3.

Masternak, Robert L. and Timothy L. Ross (1992). "Gainsharing: A Bonus Plan or Employee Involvement?" *Compensation & Benefits Review,* January-February, pp. 46-54.

McBride, Michael H. and Carolyn G. Cline (1989). "Segmenting Audiences by Type and Temperament in a Marketing Campaign," in Naomi L. Quenk (ed.) *Frontiers of Psychological Type: Proceedings of APT-VIII.* Gainesville, FL: Association for Psychological Type, pp. 123-126.

McDaid, Gerald P., Mary H. McCaulley, and Richard I. Kainz (1986). *Myers-Briggs Type Indicator Atlas of Type Tables.* Palo Alto, CA: Consulting Psychologists Press.

McKitterick, John B. (1957). "What is the Marketing Management Concept?" in Frank M. Bass (ed.) *The Frontiers of Marketing Thought and Action.* Chicago: American Marketing Association, pp. 71-82.

McQuarrie, Edward F. (1993). *Customer Visits: Building a Better Market Focus.* Newbury Park, CA: Sage Publications.

Miller, Michael W. (1987). "At Many Firms, Employees Speak a Language That's All Their Own," *Wall Street Journal,* December 29, p. 15.

Mills, Peter K. and Dennis J. Moberg (1990). "Strategic Implications of Service Technologies," in David E. Bowen et al. (eds.), *Service Management Effectiveness: Balancing Strategy, Organization and Human Resources, Operations, and Marketing.* San Francisco: Jossey-Bass, pp. 97-125.

Mitchell, Arnold (1983). *The Nine American Lifestyles: Who We Are and Where We're Going.* New York: Warner Books.

Myers, Isabel Briggs, with Peter B. Myers (1980). *Gifts Differing.* Palo Alto, CA: Consulting Psychologists Press.

Myers, Isabel Briggs and Mary H. McCaulley (1985). *Manual: A Guide to the Development and Use of the Myers-Briggs Type Indicator.* Palo Alto, CA: Consulting Psychologists Press.

Narisetti, Raju (1994). "Client Charges Consultant Sold 'Flawed' Advice," *The Wall Street Journal,* August 31, pp. B1, B5.

Novak, Thomas P. and Bruce MacEvoy (1990). "On Comparing Alternative Segmentation Schemes: The List of Values (LOV) and Values and Life Styles (VALS)," *Journal of Consumer Research,* Vol. 17, June, pp. 105-109.

Ogilvy, James (1985). *The Experience Industry.* Menlo Park, CA: SRI International.

O'Gorman, David (1993). "Chaos Theory: The New Foundation for Strategic Thought." Paper presented to the Strategic Management Society 13th Annual International Conference, September 12-15.

Ost, Edward J. (1990). "Team-Based Pay: New Wave Strategic Incentives," *Sloan Management Review,* Spring, pp. 19-27.

Ouchi, William G. and Alan L Wilkins (1985). "Organizational Culture," *Annual Review of Sociology,* XI. Palo Alto, CA: Annual Reviews, pp. 457-483.

Pacanowsky, Michael E. and Nick O'Donnell-Trujillo (1983). "Organizational Communication as Cultural Performance," *Communication Monographs,* Junc, pp. 126-147.

Paulsen, Kevin M. (1989). "Gain Sharing: A Group Motivator," *Management World,* May-June, pp. 24-25.

_______ (1991). "Lessons Learned from Gainsharing," *HR Magazine,* April, pp. 70, 72, 74.

Pearson, Andrall E. (1988). "Tough-Minded Ways to Get Innovative," *Harvard Business Review,* May-June, pp. 99-106.

Peppers, Don and Martha Rogers (1993). *The One to One Future: Building Relationships One Customer at a Time.* New York: Currency-Doubleday.

Peters, Thomas J. and Robert H. Waterman, Jr. (1982). *In Search of Excellence.* New York: Harper and Row.

Pitts, Robert E. Jr., and Arch G. Woodside (eds.) (1984). *Personal Values and Consumer Psychology.* Lexington, MA: Lexington Books.

Pranter, Charles A. and Charles L. Martin (1991). "Compatibility Management: Roles in Service Performers," *Journal of Services Marketing,* Volume 5, #2, Spring, pp. 43-53.

Pridgen, Eccles V., Jr. (1988). "(M)alice in Wonderland: Coping with Executive 'TJ' Types," Paper presented at the Ontario

Association for Psychological Type's 1st APT-Canada Conference on Psychological Type, June 3-5.

Rafiq, Mohammed and Pervaiz K. Ahmed (1993). "The Scope of Internal Marketing: Defining the Boundary Between Marketing and Human Resource Management," *Journal of Marketing Management,* Vol. 9, pp. 219-232.

Rathnam, Sukumar, Vijay Mahahan, and Andrew B. Whinston (1994). "Using Information Technology to Reduce Coordination Breakdowns in Customer Support Teams." Cambridge, MA: Marketing Science Institute, Technical Working Paper #94-105.

Rhyne, Lawrence C. (1993). "International High Technology Competition: Lessons from the America's Cup," *Proceedings* of the Third Biennial High Technology Management Conference. Boulder, CO: University of Colorado, pp. 300-309.

_______ (1994). "Product Development with a New Technology: Lessons from the America's Cup," *Journal of Product and Brand Management,* Vol. 3, #3, pp. 39-50.

Riche, Martha Farnsworth (1989). "Psychographics for the 1990's," *American Demographics,* July, pp. 24-26, 30-31, 53-54.

Ries, Al and Jack Trout (1986). *Marketing Warfare.* New York: McGraw-Hill.

Robertson, Thomas and Yoram Wind (1980). "Organizational Psychographics and Innovativeness," *Journal of Consumer Research,* Vol. 7, June, pp. 24-31.

Rogers, Everett M. (1983). *Diffusion of Innovations,* 3rd ed. New York: The Free Press.

Rokeach, Milton (1968). *Beliefs, Attitudes, and Values: A Theory of Organizations and Change.* San Francisco: Jossey-Bass.

_______ (ed.) (1979). *Understanding Human Values: Individual and Societal.* New York: The Free Press.

Ronstadt, Robert (1988). "The Corridor Principle," *Journal of Business Venturing,* Vol. 3, pp. 31-40.

Rosenfield, James R. (1994). "The Hidden Dangers of Relationship Marketing," *Direct*, October, pp. 71-76.

Ross, Timothy L. (1990). "Why Gainsharing Sometimes Fails," in Brian Graham-Moore and Timothy L. Ross (eds.), *Gain-*

sharing: Plans for Improving Performance. Washington: Bureau of National Affairs, pp. 100-115.

Saffold, Guy S. (1988). "Culture Traits, Strength, and Organizational Performance: Moving Beyond 'Strong' Culture," *Academy of Management Review,* Vol. 13, pp. 546-558.

Schein, Edgar H. (1985). *Organizational Culture and Leadership: A Dynamic View.* San Francisco: Jossey-Bass.

Schneider, Benjamin (1987). "Imperatives for the Design of Service Organizations," in Carol Surprenant (ed.), *Add Value to Your Service.* Chicago: American Marketing Association, pp. 97-99.

Schultz, Don (1994). "What Advertisers and Consumers Wanted in the Past, They Are Not Going to Want in the Future," *Link,* June, p. 44.

Sederberg, Peter C. (1984). "Organization and Explanation: New Metaphors for Old Problems," *Administration and Society,* XVI, pp. 167-194.

Senge, Peter M. (1990). *The Fifth Discipline: The Art & Practice of The Learning Organization.* New York: Doubleday.

_______ (1993). "Transforming the Practice of Management." *Human Resource Development Quarterly,* Vol. 4, #1, Spring, pp. 5-32.

Senge, Peter M., Charlotte Roberts, Richard B. Ross, Bryan J. Smith, and Art Kleinter (1994). *The Fifth Discipline Fieldbook: Strategies and Tools for Building a Learning Organization.* New York: Doubleday.

Shani, David and Sujana Chalasani (1992). "Exploiting Niches Using Relationship Marketing," *Journal of Consumer Marketing,* Vol. 9 #3, Summer, pp. 33-42.

Shanks, Donald (1985). "Profit-Oriented Customer Service." Presentation at "Markets . . . The Moving Target," A Conference sponsored by *Sales and Marketing Management* Magazine, Chicago, IL, June 12.

Siehl, Caren and Joanne Martin (1990). "Organizational Culture: A Key to Financial Performance?" in Benjamin Schneider (ed.), *Organizational Climate and Culture.* San Francisco: Jossey-Bass, pp. 241-281.

Slater, Stanley F. and John C. Narver (1993). "Market Orientation, Customer Value, and Superior Performance," Paper presented at the Third Biennial High Technology Management Conference, Boulder, CO, June 17.

Smircich, Linda (1983). "Concepts of Culture and Organizational Analysis," *Administrative Science Quarterly,* pp. 339-358.

Smith, Rolf C., Jr. (1993). "Seven Levels of Change Model: A Process for Linking Creativity, Innovation, and Continuous Improvement," in Stanley S. Gryskiewicz (ed.), *Discovering Creativity: Proceedings of the 1992 International Creativity & Innovation Networking Conference.* Greensboro, NC: Center for Creative Leadership, pp. 27-34.

Solov, Diane (1994). "Figgie Suiting Deloitte & Touche," *The* [Cleveland] *Plain Dealer,* October 12, p. C1.

Stacey, Ralph D. (1992). *Managing the Unknowable: Strategic Boundaries Between Order and Chaos in Organizations.* San Francisco: Jossey-Bass.

Staw, Barry M. (1976). "Knee Deep in the Big Muddy: A Study of Escalating Commitment to a Chosen Course of Action," *Organizational Behavior and Human Performance,* Vol. 16, p. 27.

Staw, Barry M. and Jerry Ross (1987a). "Understanding Escalation Situations: Antecedents, Prototypes, and Solutions," in L. L. Cummings and Barry M. Staw (eds.), *Research in Organizational Behavior.* Greenwich, CT: JAI Press.

_______ (1987b). "Knowing When to Pull the Plug," *Harvard Business Review,* March-April, pp. 68-74.

Tansuhaj, Patriya, Donna Randall, and Jim McCullough (1991). "Applying the Internal Marketing Concept Within Large Organizations: As Applied to a Credit Union," *Journal of Professional Services Marketing,* Volume 6, #2, pp. 193-202.

Thompson, Kenneth R. and Fred Luthans (1990). "Organizational Culture: A Behavioral Perspective," in Benjamin Schneider (ed.), *Organizational Climate and Culture.* San Francisco: Jossey-Bass, pp. 319-344.

Tilton, James (1988). Personal conversation with author.

Tobin, Daniel R. (1993). *Re-educating the Corporation: Foundations for the Learning Organization.* Essex Junction, VT: Oliver Wright Publications.

Trudel, John D. (1994). "Bottom Line: Products That Work," *Upside,* April, p. 69.

Twining, Steve (1990). "Sales Training Using the MBTI," Presented at Type and Temperament: Strength in Diversity, APT Great Lakes Region Conference, October 12.

The Type Reporter: A Quarterly Newsletter on Psychological Type (1985). Vol. 2, # 2, Fall.

United States Department of Commerce (1983). *An Assessment of United States Competitiveness in High Technology Industries*. Washington: United States Government Printing Office.

Verba, Steven M. and Dennis J. Cahill (1993). "Interactivity: The Successful Semiotics of a Product Failure," Proceedings of the Third Biennial High Technology Management Conference. Boulder, CO: University of Colorado, pp. 377-383.

Vinson, Donald E., Jerome E. Scott and Lawrence M. Lamont (1977). "The Role of Personal Values in Marketing and Consumer Behavior," *Journal of Marketing,* April, pp. 44-50.

Voss, Christopher H. (1985). "The Role of Users in the Development of Applications Software," *Journal of Product Innovation Management,* Vol. 8, pp. 113-121.

Walling, Victor C., Jr. (1984). *VALS and Innovation.* Menlo Park, CA: SRI International.

Walsh, James P. and Gerardo Rivera Ungson (1991). "Organizational Memory," *Academy of Management Review,* Vol. 16, #1, pp. 57-91.

Warrick, Brooke H. (1984). *Intellectual and Emotional Styles of the VALS Types.* Palo Alto, CA: SRI International, Inc.

Wasmer, D. J. and Gordon C. Bruner II (1991). "Using Organizational Culture to Design Internal Marketing Strategies," *The Journal of Services Marketing,* Vol. 5, #1, Winter, pp. 35-46.

Wasson, Jeanie L. (1987). "Psychographics: An Aid to Demographics," *Adweek's Marketing Week,* September 21, p. 48.

Watkins, Karen E. and Victorio J. Marsick (1993). *Sculpting the Learning Organization: Lessons in the Art and Science of Systematic Change.* San Francisco: Jossey-Bass.

Webster, Cynthia (1992). "What Kind of Marketing Culture Exists in Your Service Firm? An Audit," *Journal of Services Marketing,* Vol. 6, #2, Spring, pp. 54-67.

Webster's New World Dictionary of the American Language, College Edition (1964). Cleveland, OH: The World Publishing Company.

Wells, William D. (1975). "Psychographics: A Critical Review," *Journal of Marketing Research,* May, pp. 196-213.

Wiesendanger, Betsy (1991). "Kiosks: Automated Wonder or Lead Balloon?" *Sales and Marketing Management,* August, pp. 40-43.

Wilkins, Alan L. and W. Gibb Dyer, Jr. (1988). "Toward Culturally Sensitive Theories of Culture Change," *Academy of Management Review,* Vol. 13, pp. 522-533.

Winters, Lewis C. (1989). "New Technologies: SRI Announces VALS 2," *Marketing Research: A Magazine of Management & Applications,* June, pp. 67-69.

Yeakley, Flavil R., Jr. (1982). "Communication Style Preferences and Adjustments as an Approach for Studying Effects of Similarity in Psychological Type," *Research in Psychological Type,* Vol. 5, pp. 30-48.

_______ (1983). "Implications of Communication Style Research for Psychological Type Theory," *Research in Psychological Type,* Vol. 6, pp. 5-23.

Zenzen, Michael J. and Louis Z. Hammer (1978). "Value Measurement and Existential Wholeness: A Critique of the Rokeachean Approach to Value Research," *The Journal of Value Inquiry,* Vol. 12, #2 Spring, pp. 142-156.

Index

For Product Safety Concerns and Information please contact our EU representative GPSR@taylorandfrancis.com Taylor & Francis Verlag GmbH, Kaufingerstraße 24, 80331 München, Germany

Batch number: 10725979

Printed by Printforce, the Netherlands